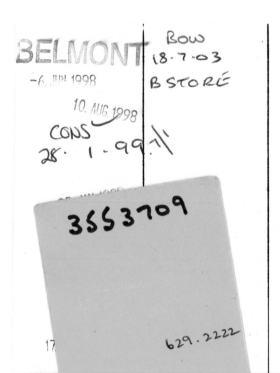

═LOTUS FILE═

=LOTUS FILE=

Seven · Elite · Elan · Europa

MARK HUGHES

TEMPLE
PRESS

© Copyright Bay View Books Ltd
First published 1987 by
Temple Press
an imprint of
The Hamlyn Publishing Group Ltd
Bridge House, London Road,
Twickenham, Middlesex TW1 3SB

Produced by Bay View Books Ltd
Bideford, Devon
Designed by Gerrard Lindley
Picture research by Jon Pressnell
Colour photography by Mick Walsh
Typeset by Atelier Dataset, St Austell
Reproduction by Isca Litho, Exeter

ISBN 0 600 55207 1
Printed in Portugal

Contents

Colour Plates

Uniquely Lotus

The cars covered in this book form the 'first generation' of Lotuses built before 1975, and all of them are distinctly different in character from the more sophisticated, up-market new Elites, Eclats, Esprits and Excels that came after them. These 'second generation' Lotuses have their following, but I suspect that even in 50 years' time the earlier models will be the ones winning the hearts of classic car enthusiasts, just as they do now.

Seven

Although the first Lotus, an Austin Seven modified for trials work, was built by Colin Chapman in 1947, the road car story began 10 years later in a flurry of excitement which saw the Seven and the Elite unveiled within months of each other. The two couldn't have been more different, with the Seven a raw, spartan, cheeky-looking little sports car designed down to a price, the Elite a highly innovative touring machine that absorbed all of Lotus's resources. Anyone at the time pontificating that the Elite would be a technical dead-end and that the engaging Seven would

still be around 30 years later would probably have been laughed at!

Sevens are uncompromising machines designed purely for spectacular performance and handling – in other words, fun. People either love them or loathe them, but anyone with a motoring soul should absolutely adore them. People who think that a good car is one that cruises along the motorway so comfortably and quietly that you don't even have to turn the radio up would hate the Seven, but thankfully there's more to motoring than that. Although it has evolved continuously, with countless engine and gearbox specifications over the years, the pure pleasures of the Seven are much as they were 30 years ago. *Sports Car Illustrated* wrote in 1958, 'After a while one becomes so used to its responsiveness that quite fantastic things can be attempted, and the Seven never fails, even if the driver's courage comes near to failing towards the end'. *Car* echoed that in 1987, saying, 'The type of progress you make is unique...what you feel, every time a wheel turns, is the sheer nimbleness of the car, its light weight, its ultra-quick steering'. *C'est la même chose...*

In 30 years the lovable Seven has gone through many identity changes from this cheeky little S1, with cyclewings up front and big 15in wheels...

Sevens as far as the eye can see at a club gathering in the late sixties: S1, S2 and S3 (from right) models are the first three in the line-up. For sheer spine-tingling driving fun the Seven is unbeatable.

...to this muscular racing version of the Caterham Super Seven. Thanks to Caterham's commitment to the Seven, today's owners are superbly catered for, regardless of the age of their Seven.

Driving a Seven is a unique experience. The buffeting from the wind, the raucous exhaust note, the jiggly ride and the liveliness of the steering all put you close to the elements, but even higher levels of exhilaration come when you start to exploit its handling. Tiny steering movements guide you through corners without a trace of roll, the neutral adhesion seeming limitless, and only with really vicious stabs of the throttle do you pro-voke the rear wheels out of line. As familiarity grows, you come to feel a part of a Seven, almost as if thought rather than muscle controls it. It becomes easy to understand why so many writers have christened the Seven the 'four-wheeled motorbike'.

There used to be a time when there was a Seven for every pocket, but now the best of the lower-priced S1s can cost nearly as much as the more brutal Caterhams, so making your choice comes down to taste. If all that matters is the joy of Seven driving, a recent or new Caterham is the wisest choice, but if you value historical significance and 'collectability' a Lotus-built car will have more appeal. On the other hand, if you can afford the best of both worlds, you could do no better than find one of the 13 S3 Twin Cam SS models, just like the glorious orange example in our colour photographs. While any of the Coventry Climax or Cosworth-tuned Super Sevens have a claim to being the definitive Seven, this one tops the lot for me. Apart from stunning handling and roadholding, the 125bhp of Holbay-tuned Twin Cam rockets this Seven over 0-60mph in 7.1secs, and only its awful aerodynamics prevent it from exceeding 100mph by a huge margin. There again, you can argue that the latest Caterham is the definitive Seven, and how many supercars of any age can beat the 170bhp Cosworth-BDR's 0-60mph in a mere 5.0secs?

Enjoy an Elite—in Safety! *The suspension system of the Elite is directly derived from that used on the fabulous Lotus Grand Prix and Sports Racing cars, giving unparalled road adhesion and comfort. The unique self-compensating properties of the Chapman Strut independent rear suspension ensure consistent handling under extreme variations of load, and Lotus rack and pinion steering gear gives faultless steering control under the most hazardous conditions of surface and 'line'.*

Elite Emergency ! *. . Feel the iron hand of the four wheel Girling Disc brakes safely sweep away all anxiety as they rush the car smoothly to rest . . .*

The Elite is tailored for travel in comfort. The thoughtfully designed seats establish new criteria for sheer luxury: cradling you restfully for all-day driving.

The wood-rimmed steering-wheel and short remote control gear-lever are arranged to reduce driver fatigue and give complete command.

Other features include matt non-reflecting dash-cowl, pile carpeting and read-at-a-glance instruments to satisfy the most critical judgment.

The Elite was a truly exceptional car, yet this sales brochure is rather low key about its abilities. Its glass-fibre monocoque structure is unique to this day, it has superb handling and braking, and an engine of only 1.2 litres can push it to nearly 120mph yet easily achieve fuel consumption of 40mpg. No wonder it's the most collectable Lotus of all today.

Sitting pretty: the Elite had the legs of its rivals when it came to beauty. The thinking behind this publicity shot was presumably that the Elite was just the car for continental tours, using the cross-channel 'air-bridge'.

Elite

If the Seven can be appreciated only by the most enthusiastic drivers, the Elite's natural owner is the complete Lotus nut. If you have yet to give into temptation and buy a Lotus, don't touch the Elite with a bargepole! For a start, rarity means that the best Elites can cost twice as much as any other classic Lotus, and when things go wrong the costs can be horrendous. None of this is to say that an Elite isn't a satisfying machine to own and drive, but it best suits the most devoted Lotus enthusiast.

Looking back from the relative greyness of eighties motoring, it is difficult to imagine a car quite so radical as the Elite being launched today, particularly by a very small manufacturer. For a start, Peter Kirwan-Taylor's styling is quite exquisite, with a pure beauty that not even the Elan can match. Underneath that flowing shape lies a glass-fibre monocoque structure which to this day remains unique: plenty of other cars have used glass-fibre bodywork, but all have possessed a metal chassis to provide structural strength. While the Elite has small steel sections bonded into its glass-fibre at a few strategic points, none of these provides its inherent rigidity, and the stresses of racing have proved the lasting qualities of this novel form of construction. Accident repair requires very specialized skills, but the scarcity of many parts and the expense of overhauling the Elite's Coventry Climax engine are the real reasons why the budding Lotus owner should cut his teeth on another model.

That said, the Elite is a gorgeous car to drive because its handling, if anything, is even better than the Elan's. The phenomenal roadholding, which is near enough neutral at normal speeds, is matched by superb all-round disc brakes, and a weight of only 13cwt means that the 1216cc Coventry Climax (producing 83bhp in the most common state of tune with twin SU carburettors) endows the Elite with sparkling performance. On the debit side it is not a flexible engine, as nothing much happens below 4000rpm, and the noise reverberating through the bodyshell can become tiring on a long journey. Lightness and an amazing drag coefficient of 0.30 (Audi thought they achieved something special with their 100 model!) give a top speed of more than 110mph – remarkable from such a small engine – and 40mpg can be obtained with ease. All in all, the Elite is a very remarkable car.

Elan

The Elan which followed in 1962 was a complete break, even though it does bear a distinct family resemblance. As the Elite's glass-fibre monocoque had been so expensive to manufacture, a steel backbone chassis with a separate glass-fibre bodyshell was adopted for the Elan, without losing any of the fine handling and roadholding qualities for which Lotus were by now renowned. Where the Elan really scored over the Elite, though, was in the performance of its 105bhp 1558cc twin-cam engine, a clever combination of Ford Cortina block and Lotus's own alloy head. Flexible and lively, this engine in its initial state of tune could push the Elan to 114mph and 0-60mph in 8.7secs, remarkable performance by the standards of the day. In its handling precision, braking efficiency and lightness of control the Elan was similar in feel to the Elite, but in ride comfort it was far superior. It managed a great leap in refinement without sacrificing any of its sporting character, and appealed to so many people that the sixties were great years for Lotus. *Motor* best summed up the Elan's qualities when it wrote, 'Just occasionally one comes across the car which is the ultimate in its chosen field; the Elan, in performance and driveability, is way ahead of all opposition in its class – the field of the true, practical fun car'.

Apart from its tremendous road behaviour, the Elan was also quite sumptuous for a sports car. All models had a wood veneer dashboard with comprehensive instrumentation, and from the S3 onwards there were

The Elan followed the Elite, but had little in common with it apart from being a fabulous driver's car. Compared with most cars, restoration is straightforward: its simple steel backbone chassis, glass-fibre body and lusty twin-cam engine do not present major difficulties, and the parts position at the factory is improving all the time. The car illustrated is a Sprint owned by Malcolm Ricketts.

even electrically-operated windows. The best car in the Elan range arrived in 1970 when Lotus's Tony Rudd developed a big-valve 126bhp version of the twin-cam. Named the Elan Sprint, this highly desirable car offered incredible performance, *Motor* recording a top speed of over 120mph and 0-60 in just 6.7secs. Not surprisingly the road tester reckoned that an Elan Sprint was one of the fastest ways of getting from A to B, and even today such performance is rare outside the exotic market.

With a total of 12,224 Elans produced in the 11 years between 1962 and 1973, no Lotus is more numerous for today's classic car buyer, and thankfully the Elan is eminently restorable. Compared with the average MG or Triumph TR, prices and restoration costs are on the high side, but from the investment point of view there are few popular sports cars to match the Elan. Everybody's favourite classic dream car after the Jaguar E-type, it seems, is a Lotus Elan. After a period in the late seventies when the factory took no interest in serving the owners of its superseded models, there are now few Elan parts that the factory cannot supply, and several independent specialists are making

reproduction items. So if you've always wanted an Elan, buy one now, while you can still afford it!

Plus 2

Lotus's desire to capture a more sophisticated market was first seen in 1967 when the 'family man's Elan', the Plus 2, was announced. Mechanically almost identical to its sister, the Plus 2 gained 12 inches in length and 7 inches in width to provide much more room for front seat occupants and space for two rear seats. Weight went up by 3cwt, but the effect on performance and handling was negligible. The motoring magazines raved more than usual, *Motor* leading the field with this verdict: 'According to our records, no other four-seater is capable of reaching 60mph in only 8.2 secs or a maximum of 125mph on a mere 1600cc...The uncanny cornering powers of this machine equal and probably exceed those of any production car we have driven before: similarly the handling and brakes are certainly not bettered'. Even though it later became known that this particular road test car had a 'tweaked' engine, the true figures were close to these.

right
A wider, longer and more refined version of the Elan, the Plus 2 was launched in 1967 and has been very popular ever since. In restoration terms it differs little from its smaller sister. In the background of this photograph, incidentally, are the transporters of Lotus's Grand Prix team.

bottom right
The little badge on the rear wing says 'S130', indicating that the 126bhp big-valve engine is fitted. This early example, without a silver roof finish, has 10-spoke Brand Lotus alloy wheels.

The S1 as first announced, bearing '1500' badges. Note the spartan door trim, how the boot lid stops short of the tail panel, and the pair of circular tail lamps. Only this convertible shape was available, but the factory did offer a hard-top.

Some improvement in creature comforts brought the Plus 2S in 1968, but this revised model was really significant in being the first Lotus that could not be bought in component form. The big-valve engine came in 1970 to create the Plus 2S130, and criticisms of its high speed cruising ability were rectified with a five-speed gearbox option a year later. Just as it did in its day, the Plus 2 nowadays appeals to the enthusiast who needs the space and likes its luxury and ride refinement, and if you want a classic Lotus for day-to-day transport this is probably the best model to go for.

Europa

All Lotuses are racing cars for the road, but perhaps the Europa, with its engine and gearbox arranged just like a Formula 1 car, is closest to this concept. Paradoxically, it has been a far less popular competition car than the Seven, Elite or Elan, and to an extent it has been less popular in the marketplace too, at least in its early days. On its launch in 1966, when it was expected to be a successor to the Seven, the Renault-powered Europa was available only on the Continent, a fact which is actually a blessing to British Lotus fans as the S1 Europa is undoubtedly the least desirable Lotus ever made! The way in which its glass-fibre body was bonded to the chassis makes it a restoration nightmare, performance from the 82bhp 1470cc Renault 16 engine is relatively gutless, and side windows that can't be opened make it ghastly to drive on a hot day.

S2 Renault Europas were rather better, but Lotus's mid-engined two-seater only gained real acceptance when the twin-cam engine was fitted in 1971. By far the best Europa is the one with the big-valve engine – this is the Special, built between 1972-75, with performance marginally better even than the Elan's. In its dynamic characteristics, however, it was definitely superior, as *Motor* confirmed with another glowing report: 'The handling and roadholding are probably as close to racing standards as you'll get anywhere in the world without buying a track car, while the ride must be the envy of many a saloon car engineer'.

These, then, are the five pre-1975 Lotuses covered in this book. Running a tatty, badly maintained example could be an enormous headache, but if you follow the guidance in the book you will hopefully find Lotus ownership a pleasure, not a pain. Lotuses in the past have suffered from unreliability, but now there are plenty of owners with carefully res-

The mid-engined Europa is a formidable performer in its ultimate Special form, but Renault-powered models are not so sparkling. Near perfect weight distribution gives it tremendous handling and roadholding, but it isn't yet quite as revered by enthusiasts as the Elan models.

tored and serviced examples to scotch that reputation.

All five are very different machines, but what they have in common is charisma, superb road manners and tremendous performance. When you drive a Lotus you are completely at one with the car. It's a sentiment repeated time and time again in road tests, but no-one has ever expressed this quality better that *Autosport*'s John Bolster when writing about the Elite in 1960: 'In Greek mythology there were gentlemen called centaurs who were half man and half horse, and I am sure that I became half Bolster and half Lotus as I flicked the Elite through the corners'. Brilliant!

PERFORMANCE FIGURES

	Seven S1 (Ford 100E engine)	Seven S2 (Super Seven 1500)	Seven S3 (Twin Cam SS Holbay)	Seven S4 (1600)	Caterham Super Seven (Lotus Twin Cam)
Max Speed	81mph	103mph	103mph	108mph	114mph
0-60mph	17.8secs	7.7secs	7.1secs	8.8secs	6.2secs
Standing ¼-mile	20.8secs	15.9secs	15.5secs	16.0secs	14.9secs
Fuel Consumption	36mpg	25mpg	19mpg	26mpg	28mpg

	Elite
Max speed	112mph
0-60mph	11.4secs
Standing ¼-mile	18.4secs
Fuel consumption	34mpg

	Elan S1	Elan S3 (Special Equipment)	Elan S4 (Special Equipment)	Elan Sprint (DHC)
Max speed	114mph	122mph	124mph	121mph
0-60mph	8.7secs	7.6secs	7.8secs	6.7secs
Standing ¼-mile	16.4secs	15.7secs	15.9secs	15.2secs
Fuel consumption	28mpg	26mpg	30mpg	26mpg

	Plus 2	Plus 2S130	Plus 2S130/5
Max speed	118mph	121mph	121mph 4th gear)
0-60mph	8.9secs	7.4secs	7.5secs
Standing ¼-mile	16.6secs	15.4secs	16.0secs
Fuel consumption	25mpg	23mpg	26mpg

	Europa S2	Europa Twin Cam	Europa Special
Max speed	110mph	117mph	122mph
0-60mph	9.5secs	7.0secs	6.6secs
Standing ¼-mile	17.3secs	15.6secs	14.9secs
Fuel consumption	30mpg	23mpg	24mpg

Seven

SPECIFICATIONS	Seven S1 (Ford 100E engine)	Seven S2 (Super Seven 1500)
Engine	In-line four	In-line four
Construction	Cast iron block and head	Cast iron block and head
Bore/stroke	63.5 x 92.5mm	80.96 x 72.7mm
Capacity	1172cc	1498cc
Valves	Sidevalves	ohv
Compression ratio	8.5:1	8.3:1
Fuel system	Single Solex carburettor	Single Weber 40DCOE carburettor
Power	40bhp at 4500rpm	66bhp at 4600rpm
Torque	58lb ft at 2600rpm	78.5lb ft at 2300rpm
Transmission	Three-speed manual	Four-speed manual
Final drive	4.875:1	4.1:1
Brakes	8in drums all round	9½in Girling discs front, 7in drums rear
Suspension front	Ind. by lower wishbones, upper links, anti-roll bar, coil springs, telescopic dampers	Ind. by lower wishbones, upper links, anti-roll bar, coil springs, telescopic dampers
Suspension rear	Live axle, twin trailing arms, diagonal link, coil springs, telescopic dampers	Live axle, twin trailing arms, A-frame, coil springs, telescopic dampers
Steering	Rack and pinion	Rack and pinion
Wheels/tyres	Bolt-on steel wheels, 5.20-15 tyres	Bolt-on steel wheels, 4.50-13 tyres
Body/chassis	Tubular steel spaceframe with aluminium panels, bonnet, wings, nosecone	Tubular steel spaceframe with aluminium panels and bonnet, glass-fibre wings and nosecone

DIMENSIONS

Length	10ft 9in	11ft 0in
Width	4ft 5in	4ft 10½in
Height	3ft 8in	3ft 7in
Wheelbase	7ft 4in	7ft 4in
Unladen weight	980lb	1036lb

NB: These details relate to one version of each series, the selection having been made to illustrate the range of specifications. All engine permutations within each series are listed at the end of this chapter.

SPECIFICATIONS

	Seven S3 (Twin Cam SS Holbay)	Seven S4 (1600)
Engine	In-line four	In-line four
Construction	Cast iron block, alloy head	Cast iron block and head
Bore/stroke	82.6 x 72.8mm	80.96 x 77.62mm
Capacity	1558cc	1598cc
Valves	Double ohc	ohv
Compression ratio	9.5:1	9.0:1
Fuel system	Twin Weber 40DCOE carburettors	Single Weber downdraught carburettor
Power	125bhp at 6200rpm	84bhp at 6500rpm
Torque	116lb ft at 4500rpm	92lb ft at 4000rpm
Transmission	Four-speed manual	Four-speed manual
Final drive	3.77:1	3.77:1
Brakes	9in Girling discs front, 8in drums rear	9in Girling discs front, 9in drums rear
Suspension front	Ind. by lower wishbones, upper links, anti-roll bar, coil springs, telescopic dampers	Ind. by lower wishbones, upper links, anti-roll bar, coil springs, telescopic dampers
Suspension rear	Live axle, twin trailing arms, A-frame, coil springs, telescopic dampers	Live axle, 'double' Watts linkage, A-frame on offside, coil springs, telescopic dampers
Steering	Rack and pinion	Rack and pinion
Wheels/tyres	Bolt-on 5½J alloy wheels, 165 x 13 tyres (195 x 13 optional)	Bolt-on 5½J steel disc wheels optional), 165 x 13 tyres
Body/chassis	Tubular steel spaceframe with aluminium panels and bonnet, glass-fibre wings and nosecone	Tubular chassis with stressed steel side panels/glass-fibre body with separate front wings and bonnet

DIMENSIONS

Length	11ft 1in	12ft 0½in
Width	5ft 1in	5ft 0in
Height	3ft 1in	3ft 7½in
Wheelbase	7ft 5in	7ft 6in
Unladen weight	1258lb	1276lb

SPECIFICATIONS

Caterham Super Seven (Lotus Twin Cam)

Engine	In-line four
Construction	Cast iron block, alloy head
Bore/stroke	82.6 x 72.8mm
Capacity	1558cc
Valves	Double ohc
Compression ratio	10.3:1
Fuel system	Twin Dell'Orto carburettors
Power	126bhp at 6500rpm
Torque	113lb ft at 5500rpm
Transmission	Four-speed manual
Final drive	3.89:1
Brakes	9in Girling discs front, 8in drums rear
Suspension front	Ind. by lower wishbones, upper links, anti-roll bar, coil springs, telescopic dampers
Suspension rear	Live axle, twin trailing arms, A-bracket, coil springs, telescopic dampers
Steering	Rack and pinion
Wheels/tyres	Bolt-on 5½J alloy wheels, 165 x 13 tyres
Body/chassis	Tubular steel spaceframe with aluminium panels and bonnet, glass-fibre wings and nosecone

DIMENSIONS

Length	10ft 11in
Width	5ft 1in
Height	3ft 1in
Wheelbase	7ft 5in
Unladen weight	1162lb

What do we do now? The most popular of the Lotus-built Sevens was the S2 offered between 1960-68, and the vast majority were sold in component form. The dream of every Seven enthusiast is to find one still in its boxes today.

Thirty years have passed since Colin Chapman conceived the Lotus Seven as a 'bargain basement' sports car offering good performance and sensational handling. At the time it was a poor relation in Lotus plans compared with racing car manufacture and the gestation of the radical new Elite, and throughout the 16 years of Lotus production prior to Caterham's takeover of manufacturing rights in 1973 it remained so. Only during the Caterham era, it seems, has the fate of the Seven been truly secure.

So it was that Lotus never took much interest in the Seven, expending effort on minimal development only when time allowed. The most devoted enthusiasts, however, took the Seven to their hearts, and the cult following for this 'four-wheeled motorbike' is stronger today than ever before. Regardless of whether you are tempted by a brand new

For the first two years all Sevens were built with the venerable Ford sidevalve 1172cc engine, shown here with optional twin SU carburettors.

Caterham or an S1 'basket case', there's no doubt that you would be hard pushed to buy more fun for your money.

Engine

Never has there been a car with such a bewildering range of engine specifications as the Seven. All told, there have been 18 different units of various makes, capacities and tune, ranging from the 37bhp 948cc BMC A-series to the 170bhp Ford-Cosworth BDR, and Caterham's policy of continuous development will bring further powerplants in the future. On top of this, the Seven's raw excitement has always made it a favourite candidate for the home tuner, so many cars have been modified over the years, and some have even received transplants with such unlikely engines as the Alfa Romeo twin-cam or the Rover V8. While the power to weight ratio of the latter would be pretty appealing, you should make original specification your number one rule of thumb. Apart from the fact that the most original cars are also the most desirable and valuable, a car that has been excessively tampered with could cause all sorts of maintenance and safety problems.

That said, most of the engines used in Sevens over the years are very robust, and none more so than the Ford units which powered the majority of Lotus-built Sevens. Upon the Series 1's launch in October 1957, the 1172cc sidevalve Ford 100E engine (with pre-war origins!) was the standard fitment, albeit with a number of performance options such as twin SU carburettors and a special exhaust manifold. The performance of this archaic but rugged engine wasn't terribly spirited, so many S1s have been 'up-engined' to later Ford units, making an original sidevalve S1 a very rare beast. If you can find one, don't worry too much about engine shortcomings as it will take a long time to find another! Although inherently reliable, these engines don't have a very long life, becoming tired after as little as 30,000 miles, but most parts are still available through the Ford Sidevalve Owners Club and there are plenty of Ford Populars, Prefects and Anglias languishing in scrapyards. As long as smoke isn't pouring out of the exhaust, there aren't any oil leaks, the oil and coolant look clean, the engine runs well and doesn't overheat, there should be nothing to worry about.

In late 1958, Lotus answered the need for more power by fitting the Coventry Climax FWA all-aluminium 1098cc overhead camshaft engine to the Super Seven, transforming the performance with 75bhp compared with the Ford's 40bhp. These cars are also rare – quite how rare no-one knows because production figure information for Sevens is so patchy – but at least most of those built have remained close to original specification. When examining one of these cars it's important to satisfy yourself that the owner has maintained it carefully as the Climax engine needs very regular attention. Signs of the slapdash owner are low oil level (only 200 miles per pint is the typical consumption), damaged threads on the cylinder head bolts (it is common for inexperienced mechanics to tighten down the head way beyond its low torque wrench settings) and overheating (internal corrosion on an aluminium engine can clog the waterways and radiator if an inhibitor has not been added to the coolant). There should be no exhaust smoke, no signs of water in the oil (or oil in the water) and no irregular sounds from what is a noisy engine anyway. A compression check is strongly advised to detect any valve or piston problems. There are few parts difficulties as the number of these engines still being raced has helped to maintain spares availability, but you must bear in mind that it is extremely expensive to overhaul a Coventry Climax. With

most 'run of the mill' Sevens engine condition is not the top consideration – with the Super Seven it is, so do seek a specialist's confirmation if you think you've found a good car. If there are obvious and major engine problems, don't touch the car unless you really know what you're doing, and make sure that the cost of repair is reflected in the purchase price.

The third type of engine found in S1 Sevens is the 948cc BMC A-series unit used in the Austin A35, Morris Minor and 'Frog-eye' Sprite, and introduced by Lotus in October 1959 mainly with a view to the American market (where the car was named the Seven America). Although marginally inferior to the sidevalve Ford on top-end power, the A-series is just as willing low-down and revs quite sweetly. Few engines are quite as rugged and durable, 90,000 miles being a typical life-span, and they tolerate infrequent maintenance very well. Don't be put off by a rattling timing chain as this a common ailment which need not mean imminent breakage, but will require renewal. Make the usual checks and all should be well, and don't worry if there are problems – as with Ford sidevalve engines – since these Sevens are rare and all engine spares can be found, by cannibalizing Minors or A35s if necessary.

Many Ford and BMC engines were modified by their owners, perhaps with racing in mind, so it is unusual now to find an S1 in 'from the factory' condition. Just how it has been modified will probably have been lost in the mists of time, but non-standard carburettors could be a sign that the engine's internals have been changed too, using tuning parts which were common at the time – steel crankshafts and con rods, higher-lift camshafts and so on. You can't take the engine apart in the vendor's drive, so you will have to rely on what you can see, the feel of the engine during your road test and the owner's word. With all three S1 engines, it is quite likely that an electric cooling fan will have been fitted as overheating in traffic was common with the standard engine-driven fan.

The S2 Seven arrived in June 1960, at first only with the same BMC A-series – fitted to most of the early cars – and Ford sidevalve engines. Chassis changes precluded the use of the Coventry Climax in the S2, but this had been an expensive engine in any case and an alternative was in the pipeline. Far more common, however, are Sevens powered by the Ford Anglia 105E 997cc ohv engine, which was introduced by Lotus early in 1961 and remained the basic model's power unit for seven years. Rather smoother than the

The S2 brought sweeping glass-fibre wings, smaller 13in wheels and some lightening of the chassis. The simple windscreen style inherited from the S1 has remained to this day, but those wipers were new as a standard fitting.

The name 'Cosworth' cast into the rocker cover gives the game away. This is an S2 Super Seven with a Cosworth-modified 1340cc Ford Classic 109E engine breathing through twin Weber carburettors. It can push the Seven's brick-like profile to over 100mph.

A-series, the 105E offered similar performance which was reasonable for its day but modest now. One aspect of this engine is spectacular – its durability. Go through your check procedure in the usual way, and don't be surprised if all seems well. These engines have no real weaknesses, and can happily exceed 100,000 miles if not driven too hard. Parts, once again, are readily available from motor factors or through the Ford 105E Owners Club.

Through the first year of S2 production, the lack of a 'flier' in the range was a problem, but the appearance of a new Super Seven in July 1961 rectified this. Yet another humble Ford saloon engine, this time the ohv 1340cc 109E from the Classic, provided the basis for the quickest Seven yet, but it took Cosworth modifications to make it so. Instantly recognizable from the Cosworth name cast into the rocker cover, these engines have twin Weber carburettors, a four branch manifold, a Cosworth camshaft and cylinder head modification to produce a smooth power delivery, peaking at 85bhp. As a result, the S2 Super Seven is one of the most desirable of the Lotus-built Sevens.

Unfortunately, it also presents more mechanical problems, largely because the capacity gain over the 997cc engine was achieved entirely by taking the stroke out from 48.4mm to 65.0mm, thereby putting excessive strain on the centre main bearing of the three-bearing crankshaft. Even in standard form in the Ford Classic, the crank's 'whip' destroyed the centre bearing quite early in life, so the problems with the Cosworth version, where all the modifications were to the head, can be imagined. Main bearings have a short life, and high revving can even cause the crank to snap.

The final Ford engine used in the S2 doesn't share these problems, for the ohv 1498cc 116E from the Cortina had a five-bearing crankshaft. This power unit arrived with the Super Seven 1500 in September 1962 and was usually sold in 66bhp standard form with a single Weber sidedraught carburettor mounted on Lotus's own inlet manifold. Cosworth set to work on this engine too, extracting 95bhp with similar cylinder head

work, higher compression and twin Weber 40DCOE carburettors. Once again, these Ford engines are extremely reliable, even in Cosworth tune, and it is unlikely that the usual checks will yield anything more serious than timing chain or rocker shaft noise. Oil pressure should be at least 40psi at 3000rpm and 20psi at tickover. Twin Webers have been added to quite a few standard tune cars, and any 'missing' at tickover or sluggishness in performance could be due to these needing adjustment. These engines generally last 100,000 miles before needing major attention, and even then all parts are available and overhaul is not too expensive. Late-model Cosworth 1500s don't have Cosworth rocker covers.

Ford's new crossflow 225E 'Kent' engine arrived with the S3 in August 1968, Lotus offering it in 1598cc and 1297cc variants – the former is far more common. Developing 84bhp with a single Weber downdraught carburettor, the 1598cc in standard form was nearly as powerful as earlier tuned 1500s, and offered new scope for tuning. Its crossflow cylinder head, with the exhaust and inlet manifolds mounted on opposite sides of the engine, was the major difference compared with the 116E. You are quite likely to find tuning modifications (with parts generally supplied by Holbay because of a tie-up with Lotus to supply Formula Ford engines), but there are no special problems other than the camshaft and valve gear wear that develops with frequent high revving – just listen for excessive noise in these areas. Otherwise, the Kent is a very durable unit engineered with plenty of strength margin, and is still being used by Ford today. Needless to say, all parts are available. Full Holbay specification engines (in the Seven S) produce a very healthy 120bhp, thanks to engine balancing, a high-lift camshaft, gas-flowed cylinder head, new pistons (giving a 10.0:1 compression ratio), new exhaust and inlet manifolds and twin Weber 40DCOE carburettors.

This same engine, usually in standard 1598cc form, powered the bulk of S4s, and became the mainstay of Caterham production after supplies of Lotus and Vegantune twincams became short. Caterham have built many cars with the Kent engine in standard 84bhp guise, while the tuned version which was really needed to come near the performance of Lotus twin-cam cars arrived in 1980. Named the 'Sprint', it heralded what could be called a second generation of Caterham production, where twin-cam performance could be offered at lower cost. By gas-flowing the head using a Newman A2 camshaft, and fit-

ting twin Weber carburettors on a Holbay manifold, Caterham managed to extract 110bhp without sacrificing the engine's smooth and untemperamental character. Further tuning work by Peter Cooper produced 135bhp for the 'Supersprint' version, bored out to 1698cc, and in this form the Caterham Super Seven performs better than any of the twin-cam models.

All through S2 and S3 production, Lotus's fabulous twin-cam engine had been powering the Elan, but the Seven had been so far down the list of priorities (the Elan was developed, and the Europa and Plus 2 launched, during this period) that the factory never got round to giving it this engine, offering the excuse that it wouldn't fit. Caterham's Graham Nearn, however, showed the factory a Seven into which one of his customers had fitted a twin-cam, and so the Twin Cam SS was born. It is without doubt the most desirable and quickest of all Lotus-built Sevens, and rarity – only 13 are thought to have been built – enhances its attraction. All had Holbay-assembled versions of the twin-cam producing 125bhp, and the chassis was strengthened to cope.

The unloved S4 was fitted with the twin-cam from the beginning, in 115bhp and Holbay-tuned 125bhp forms (alongside Ford 1598cc and a handful of 1297cc versions). When Caterham bought the rights to the Seven in 1973 and set about returning to S3 manufacture, it made sense to offer the twin-cam in 126bhp big-valve form in their car – when launched in September 1974 it set a new performance benchmark for the Seven of 0-60mph in 6.2secs. All early Caterham S3s were made to this specification, but within two years supplies of the Lotus twin-cam dried up, the engine no longer being used in Lotus road cars after the Europa Special was discontinued in 1975. Most Sevens built in 1977-78, therefore, have twin-cams assembled by Vegantune from kits of parts supplied by Lotus.

A further threat to supply came when Lotus ran out of engine cranks. As the twin-cam block was a Ford 116E item bored out to 1558cc, it was a relatively straightforward task for Vegantune to take the larger 1598cc 225E block and mate the alloy twin-cam head to it. Producing exactly the same power output as the normal twin-cam, this 'tall-block' conversion allowed more engines to be made until cylinder heads became unavailable. These supply difficulties pushed Caterham back to those modified Kent engines for the bulk of production, but the twin-cam enjoyed a final swansong when Vegantune built a new

130bhp version, still based on the Kent but with a new head design employing belt-driven double overhead camshafts. Designated the VTA, it was installed in 30 Sevens during 1979-80.

Far more care needs to be taken when inspecting a Seven with a twin-cam engine because overhaul is more expensive than for any of the pure Ford engines, and cylinder heads are as rare as hen's teeth. Read the engine section of the Elan chapter for the full details, but suffice to say here that blue exhaust smoke on acceleration will mean that a bottom-end rebuild is imminent and smoke when lifting off will probably mean worn valve guides. There should be no oil leaks, oil pressure should be 36psi at 3000rpm, and the timing chain should not be noisy. This last point is a common twin-cam problem, and a breakage has dire results on valves and pistons – if the adjuster on the inlet side of the engine is screwed fully home it is time for a new chain. Twin-cams also have a history of water pump failure – make sure that the fan belt is not too tight, as this is the usual cause. In short, twin-cams are very reliable if they're properly rebuilt and maintained, but any smoke or oil leaks will mean some large bills ahead.

Gearbox and rear axle

Gearbox changes through the life of the Seven were not quite so frequent as the upgrading of engines, and once again most are of Ford origin – this is good news for today's Seven buyer or restorer, as parts for all but the earliest 'boxes are cheap and available.

From our viewpoint in the eighties, when most new cars have five-speed gearboxes, the fact that the first sidevalve S1s had a three-speed 'box makes them seem awfully old! It has a light change, but you must be careful to cross the gate firmly from first (which has no synchromesh) to second to avoid 'snicking' reverse. This is quite a strong gearbox, but second has to work so hard that its synchromesh is likely to have worn, and the lever may even jump out of gear. Any gearbox problems can be solved by raiding a scrapped 100E Anglia, Prefect or Popular. The differential of these Ford S1s consisted of a Nash Metropolitan rear axle with a standard final drive of 4.8:1 (although other ratios were available), and compared with later Sevens these are quite durable. Replacements can't be found now, so any oil leaks or looseness in the driveline will again eventually require a visit to a scrapyard.

Although the Coventry Climax S1 Super Seven in prototype form was given a Lotus Eleven de Dion rear end, production models kept the same Nash Metropolitan back axle with a taller 4.55:1 ratio to increase top speed. The gearbox, however, was a four-speed from the Austin A30 with close ratio gears, which also featured when the Seven A was introduced in late 1959. These 'boxes are very rugged, and even when first gear typically starts to whine and synchromesh weakens they still have quite a bit of life left. If the car you inspect has a particularly tired 'box, fear not since reconditioned units are readily available.

BMC and Ford-powered S2s have the same gearbox alternatives, but the by now obsolete Nash Metropolitan axle was replaced by one from the Standard Eight, even though that was close to being phased out. As the 105E, 109E and 116E Ford engines were progressively introduced, so the appropriate gearboxes from Anglia, Classic and Cortina were installed, all of these being very robust four-speed units. Only the Cortina 'box has synchromesh on first gear. You are unlikely to find any gearbox problems, but if you do new and scrapyard parts are available.

In contrast, the Standard rear axle is a notorious trouble spot on S2 Sevens. Designed by Standard for a maximum power output of around 40bhp, this rear axle seemed fine for the relatively weak-kneed early Sevens, but by the time Cosworth versions of the 1340cc and 1498cc engines were pumping out 85bhp and 95bhp it just wasn't man enough for the job. The problem really stemmed from Chapman's A-frame rear suspension which attached at its rearward apex to a lug on the lower side of the differential housing. On the most powerful cars, and specially those fitted with wider tyres than standard, the suspension stresses which were fed into the axle casing caused the differential mounting nuts to work loose and oil to leak. The rubber bushes locating the A-frame to the axle would then perish as they became subjected to oil, the suspension would start to vibrate on its mountings and the stresses would grow. The eventual result was that the axle casing would split.

The solution to all this is some form of bracing which spreads the loads along the width of the axle, and most S2s now have strengthening. A Caterham man, Ron Davies, designed a quarter-plate reinforcing brace which went all the way round the back of the diff housing and tapered out along the axle casing. Caterham put the idea to Lotus,

who introduced it on the last of the S2s. When you look at an S2 rear axle, check that a brace – preferably one that extends the whole length of the axle – has been fitted, and that there are no major oil leaks to hint at future problems. As new Standard axles are no longer available, a good few cars have received Ford Escort axle transplants (together with S3 Ford front hubs to keep the wheel centres the same). These are far stronger, but sticklers for originality should go for a car with a braced Standard axle.

Ford Escort Mexico rear axles arrived with the S3s, but a small penalty of their extra strength was an increase in unsprung weight. Lotus didn't bother to fit any bracing, and exactly the same differential flexing tended to happen, albeit later in the car's life. Not such a large proportion of S3s have bracing, and unless you are looking at a Holbay-tuned 225E engine or Twin Cam SS its absence merely means that previous owners have not found it necessary (probably by not driving the car hard, so you could almost look at it as a plus point!). Should you find a car with a noisy or leaking axle, new units can still be found at some Ford dealers, and reconditioned or used items can easily be obtained. The dependable Cortina gearbox – by now Ford were acknowledged to be mak-

This diagram indicates the main areas of chassis fatigue on the S2: the A-frame mounting below the differential and suspension pick-up points must be examined. The shaded area represents the bracing with which most S2s have been fitted to ease the loading on the differential casing.

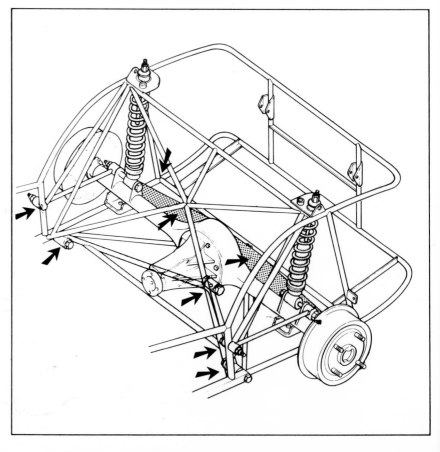

ing just about the best 'boxes in the world – remained. The Ford Escort axle continued to be used on the S4, on which revised Watts linkage suspension meant that it gives no problems. Yet another gearbox, that from the Corsair 2000E, appeared, and you shouldn't find anything to worry about with this either.

As Caterham at first continued to use the Escort axle, the brace was fitted to all their early S3s with the big-valve twin-cam engine, and occasionally its power has caused the axle casing to break where the brace ends. The vulnerable A-frame mounting had been protected, but the radius arms were now loading and cracking the outer ends of the axle casing. As a result, the brace was extended right across the axle, and ideally any early Caterham Seven you inspect should have this modification – thus equipped, the Escort axle is unbreakable. RS2000 rear axles were used for a short period, and since 1980 all live axle cars have had BL's strong Morris Ital item. The most recent de Dion suspended cars have a Ford Sierra differential with 3.6:1 final drive. Gearboxes have remained Ford items throughout, the Escort Sport having replaced the 2000E Corsair unit in 1981, and the Ford Sierra five-speed having lately become an option. All these drivetrains are extremely robust, and you are unlikely to find any whine or clonks in the system.

Suspension, steering and brakes

In its basic suspension design, the Seven has remained fundamentally unchanged in 30 years, with a traditional combination of independent front and live axle rear suspension. The only exceptions are a handful of early prototype and customer-modified cars using the Lotus Eleven's de Dion rear layout, and a de Dion option in the Caterham range since 1985.

The front suspension of the S1 was identical to that of the 'high-tech' Elite introduced in the same year, using an economical arrangement whereby a pair of upper links created the top wishbone, the leading link on each side being formed from the ends of an anti-roll bar. A conventional lower wishbone, Hillman uprights and integral coil spring and telescopic damper units completed the picture. At the rear, the live axle was supported by twin trailing arms, and a single diagonal tube from the offside end of the axle to the back of the transmission tunnel looked after

lateral location. The earliest cars had a Burman worm and nut steering box mounted behind the front wheel centre line, but its vagueness soon brought a modified Morris Minor rack set in the same position. While disc brakes were part of the expensive Elite's specification, the featherweight and cheap Seven made do with perfectly adequate 8in Girling drums (as used by Ford) all round, sitting within large 15in steel disc wheels. All in all, the suspension was an economical mixture of largely proprietory parts fitted together to follow racing practice.

Quite a few significant changes were made for the S2 at both front and rear. At the front Triumph Herald uprights and steering rack were adopted, the rack now being mounted ahead of the wheel centre line to give more foot room around the pedals and eliminate the need for universal joints in the steering column. The change to Triumph hubs (of smaller diameter) was matched at the back by the use of that infamous Standard rear axle. At the rear an A-frame bolting on to the bottom of the differential casing and a straight radius arm on each side provided the location. Spring/damper units shared the radius arm mounting points on top of the axle. Smaller 13in steel wheels all round gave a slightly less ungainly appearance, and the Standard rear drum brakes were smaller at 7in diameter. With the Super Seven 1500 came 9½in front disc brakes (from the Triumph Spitfire) to give greater stopping power.

Further changes were made to go with the S3's new Ford rear axle and hubs, special front hub assemblies having to be commissioned to match. Ford's 5½J Cortina steel wheels were now fitted all round (although the 'hot' Holbay-tuned models had Brand Lotus alloy rims), the front disc brakes of the S2 Super Seven 1500 were standard across the board, and rear drum size (Ford components now, of course) returned to 8in.

With the S4 came a completely new rear suspension layout aimed to overcome those axle breakages. In place of the A-frame were two Watts linkages with the top arms running rearwards and the bottom arms connecting forwards to the chassis – spring/damper units were now arranged as Chapman struts. In the manner of the S1, a triangulated arm on the offside took care of lateral location. Front suspension remained a double wishbone arrangement, but now used the pressed steel wishbones of the Europa (without an anti-roll bar) in place of the tubular components of all the earlier Sevens. Brakes didn't change, but the S2/S3 Herald steering rack was replaced

above
S3 Sevens — upon which Caterham's Seven is based — are at first sight identical to S2s, but look carefully and you will spot the broader rear wheel arches required to accommodate the wider track of the Ford Escort axle, which replaced the S2's obsolete and troublesome Standard axle.

Every prospective Seven purchaser must have his favourite, but high on anyone's shopping list must be the S2 Super Seven, with an 80bhp Cosworth-tuned 109E Ford engine. This gorgeous example is owned by Malcolm Ricketts.

Vincent Haydon's Twin Cam SS, with just 20,000 miles on the clock and entirely original in specification, must be one of the most desirable of all the myriad Sevens.

Autocar *said of this Seven: 'One of that in terms of vulnerability, comfort, control, performance and sheer enjoyment, the Lotus Seven Twin Cam SS is a four-wheeled motorbike…those of us who drove it found it most satisfying'.*

The five very different types of 'first generation' Lotuses covered in this book, from the raw performances of the Seven to the refined capability of the Plus 2. There's almost a Lotus for all tastes.

inset *The Holbay-tuned twin-cam delivers 125bhp, enough to catapult this 11cwt little slingshot over 0-60mph in just 7.1secs, and on to a top speed of 103mph.*

A picture of one of the most exquisite driving experiences: a Lotus Seven and an open road at twilight.

There's no doubt that the S4's styling was a retrograde step from the functional looks of earlier Sevens, but it was intended to be a more civilized car that would appeal to a new type of buyer. With nearly 900 built in three years, the S4 took Seven production levels to a new peak.

by a Burman rack and pinion system and Triumph collapsible steering column. Brakes were 9in discs at the front, 9in drums at the rear.

Caterham-built cars are identical in layout to the S3, but there have been a few running changes to suit new component suppliers. Mini-based steering replaced the Herald rack in 1983, BL brakes came with the Ital axle in 1981, and de Dion rear suspension became an option in 1985.

Although the suspension is not a weak point on Sevens, it should be checked carefully as poor handling defeats the whole point of owning a Seven! You can learn an awful lot on your test drive once you know how a good Seven feels, and any sloppiness in the handling, any pull or vagueness in the steering, or noises from the suspension, warrant closer examination. That said, if a car you inspect doesn't feel right the chances are that chassis damage or fatigue is the real cause. This is all dealt with in the next section, so don't immediately suspect the suspension if it

appears to be sound. Rock the car at each corner to check damper condition, and make sure that all the rubber bushing is in good shape. Perished bushes in extreme cases will make themselves felt behind the wheel and you may hear the suspension chattering because of loose metal-to-metal contact. If this condition is at all severe, evidenced visually by wear in the joints, you will need to pay particular attention to the chassis around the suspension pick-ups. Irregular tyre wear will mean that you must check the tracking, and again you could find that the chassis is responsible. On S2 and S3 cars in particular, make sure that the crucial A-frame rubber bush below the differential casing is sound.

The steering should be light, quick and precise, but the brakes do require fairly strong pedal pressure. If there is any lost motion in the steering a new rack is the likely remedy, and any pulling from the brakes suggests that a simple overhaul is necessary. None of this presents any worries as all these proprietory parts can be obtained.

Body and Chassis

All Sevens apart from the S4 have a very light spaceframe formed from 18swg steel tubing of 1in and ¾in diameter, and the state of this minimal chassis (it can easily be lifted by two men) is crucial to the safety and handling. Throughout the life of the Seven, minor changes have been made to the chassis to suit different engines and to strengthen points of weakness.

The strength of the S1 chassis is helped by its bodywork, made entirely of aluminium, being riveted to the spaceframe where possible, such as along the side panels, floorpan (which extended to the full length under the engine and boot) and propshaft tunnel. Dzus fasteners locate the nosecone, and the one-piece aluminium bonnet can be lifted right off for access to the engine. The most distinctive aspect of the S1's appearance is the cycle wing type front mudguards, which attach to the spaceframe by rigid stays so that they don't turn with the wheels.

American regulations brought flared wings for S1s bound for that market, and these glass-fibre items were fitted to the S2 to give it a much more rakish look. But there were far more significant changes under the surface to make the chassis simpler and cheaper to build, and to remove some of the inconsistencies in dimensions. Knowing that the riveted aluminium skins provided extra rigidity, Colin Chapman dispensed with diagonal tubes in the engine bay and cockpit sides, and the new A-frame rear suspension allowed the steel hoop around the back of the transmission tunnel (previously a suspension pick-up point) to be removed. The undertray was shortened to just the cockpit area, and the dashboard was now riveted to form a bulkhead. As well as the wings, the nosecone was also made of self-coloured glass-fibre (for economy), and the radiator cap no longer protruded through it. The S2 was also made slightly more civilized a year after its launch when sidescreens were offered for the first time. During the life of the S2, chassis con-

Isn't it basic? This shot of an S1 shows part of the economical tubular steel spaceframe chassis, which has remained fundamentally unchanged to this day, and the live axle (in this case an Austin Metropolitan item).

Chassis gradually receiving their running gear at Caterham's production line. Aluminium panelling is riveted to the tubular structure.

struction, which had always been contracted out (first to Progress Chassis and then Universal Radiators), was finally taken on by Arch Motors, with whom it remains to this day.

No significant bodywork or chassis changes were made when the S3 was launched, but as more and more power became installed in the Seven so chassis inadequacies were beginning to appear on customer cars. The creation of the Twin Cam SS was the prompting Lotus needed to start putting back the engine bay and cockpit side triangulation removed from the S2. Although the Twin Cam SS is the only Lotus-built S3 with these added chassis tubes, all Caterham-built S3s to date have followed these principles, along with other modifications. Right from the beginning, for example, Caterham have fitted a reinforcing steel plate to the transmission tunnel around the gearbox mounting to counter the flexing that used to cause the aluminium rivets to work loose. The major changes came in 1981 with a long-cockpit

version for taller drivers, achieved by shifting the rear seat panel back by 2½in and moving some chassis tubes to accommodate it, and in 1984 on the de Dion prototype car with additional tubes along the sides of the transmission tunnel (these were then incorporated on all Caterham chassis).

To quote Caterham's David Wakefield, 'The spaceframe has known weak points in certain areas after lengthy service.' With the Lotus philosophy of 'adding lightness', S2 and S3 Sevens have the most flexible chassis, and there are a couple of places where suspension stresses (particularly on the higher powered cars) can cause fatigue, and ultimately fracture. One vulnerable point that you must examine is where the rear axle radius arms meet the chassis, the mounting being a metal sleeve welded into a vertical tube. When the rear axle radius arms pivot they put strain on this tube, and as the retaining bolts work loose they move around and cause further stress. If allowed to deteriorate, these mountings eventually pull away from the chassis, and if this happens in the middle of a fast corner you could be in trouble! There is an additional diagonal tube on Caterham Sevens to dissipate this loading, and you may find a car with other DIY evidence of strengthening. Look also at the front around the suspension pick-ups and steering rack mountings for evidence of the same stresses. Even if you can't see anything amiss, be very wary of a car with damaged suspension mountings or badly worn bushes – in time the chassis tubes could start to open up.

It is essential to check that all the chassis tubes are true, but unless you are a real Seven expert you are unlikely to notice anything wrong. Here, more than in any other aspect of buying a Seven, professional knowledge in the form of a specialist inspection could save you from buying a lemon. One of the beauties of the Seven chassis is that most of it can be seen easily. It's fair to say that very few cars have a completely untouched original chassis, but at the same time completely new chassis are rare too. Serious chassis derangement should be obvious, and in any case would influence the car's road behaviour, but minor accident damage, fatigue or amateur repairs may well be missed by a layman. There are plenty of Seven owners who have bought privately and learned the hard way, so be warned! None of these problems is a reason to reject a car, as chassis repair is relatively straightforward and almost inevitable one day, but they should certainly affect the price.

Corrosion is really not a problem on the stove-enamelled tubular structure. There will probably be chipped paint where the engine and gearbox have been taken out, and surface rust on lower parts of the chassis, but all the tubes are made of a heavy gauge steel which hardly ever rusts right through.

You should look for a chassis plate to confirm that a car is really what it purports to be (all the known details are listed in the production history appendix), although some Lotus-built cars have lost their chassis plates. The plate is mounted under the bonnet on the horizontal bulkhead. On Lotus-built cars with windscreen washers, the water bottle is secured by an elastic strap right over the chassis plate, and you may find that years of rubbing have removed all the details! If you can't prove a car's identity by chassis plate, the type of rear axle, engine, chassis and so on should all tie in with the specifications discussed so far. Just to throw a spanner in the works, though, the S1 that has received a new S2 chassis (it's not unknown) and an up-

dated engine really does have an identity problem!

Bodywork on S2, S3 and Caterham Sevens should cause no problems, because all the glass-fibre panels are available to replace damaged sections. The S1's aluminium panelling can be re-made (by Williams & Pritchard, the original manufacturers, among others), but replacing a damaged nosecone will be expensive. The ready availability of glass-fibre panels has meant that many S1s are no longer strictly original – it's quite common to find them fitted with S2-type glass-fibre nosecones and flared wings. If you do find any bodywork damage, treat it as a negotiating point.

That piece of advice doesn't hold quite so true for the S4 Seven, for its construction is totally different. In producing a 'civilized Seven', Lotus design personnel (reputedly without Chapman's knowledge) developed a simpler spaceframe relying on spot-welded flat steel panels along the cockpit and engine bay sides for part of its strength. Onto this frame was dropped a single-piece outer skin. Front wings and bonnet panels were separate, but the rear wings were integral with this bodyshell, which contained bobbins at the chassis mounting points. Unlike all other Sevens, this bodyshell also provided some of the car's strength.

This steel chassis is particularly prone to corrosion, and it could be that the car you examine – if you really want an S4! – is being sold because the owner knows that its chassis life is limited. A sloppy feel on your road test will indicate that the chassis and bodyshell need the most thorough examination. In the past the lower value of S4s has made fewer people inclined to pay for a new chassis, but values have crept up now to the point where a chassis change can be cost-effective.

The problems have arisen, of course, because so much of the chassis is made of sheet steel, and the tray where the front suspension and steering rack are mounted and the rear suspension pick-up points are particularly vulnerable areas. The front suspension tray is easily visible under the bonnet, and you might find that filler and fresh paint have been used to cover up corrosion horrors. If this area has been 'got at', the rear part of the frame is going to be in the same condition. Where tubes and steel panels meet there are appalling mud traps, and many of these areas are very inaccessible because the glass-fibre shell drops over the chassis. Although you can't check these hidden areas, the extent of corrosion will be obvious from the exposed side panels.

The S4 has a small luggage compartment at the back, an improved hood, a roll-over bar and sensible new sidescreens with sliding perspex windows.

Cutaway drawing of the S4, which nobody seems to love. Entirely new glass-fibre bodywork and a tubular spaceframe/sheet steel chassis made it a complete break with Seven tradition.

As the S4 has a single-piece glass-fibre bodyshell, any bodywork shortcomings are costly to rectify. If the self-colouring has deteriorated to the point where it looks patchy or 'milky', it will need to be resprayed in the conventional glass-fibre fashion, which means laborious stripping back, filling, flatting and repainting. Any damaged areas will need to be replaced by new sections (this is really a job for a professional), and you will probably end up having a full respray. Only the smallest chips and scratches can be repaired with self-coloured gel. You must look for stress cracks in the gel coat as these will also mean an expensive respray. As a footnote, Caterham-built S4s had their own redesign of the Lotus badge, but many owners have fitted Lotus badges – the chassis number will confirm identity.

Interior

This will be a short section, for two reasons: the Seven doesn't have a great deal of interior, and as a potential Seven owner you have already decided that creature comfort is not one of your priorities! Mind you, today's Caterhams are poles apart from the spartan S1, and the whole of Seven evolution has seen little-by-little attempts to improve comfort and equipment levels.

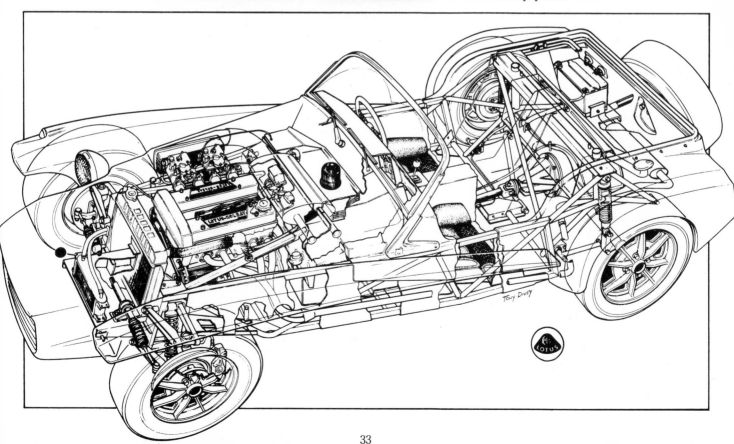

The 1216cc all-alloy Coventry Climax engine usually came with single or twin SU carburettors, but Miles Wilkins' car has the twin Webers found on the rare Super 95, 100 and 105 models.

Elite's interior, designed by Peter Cambridge, is functional yet stylish.

Like all the Lotuses covered in this book, the Elite was available in component form to beat purchase tax. It looks like a giant plastic kit, which is really just what it was.

Gearbox and rear axle

The Elite's use of proprietory components continues in the transmission areas. The four-speed gearbox of the S1 was lifted straight from the earliest of the MGAs, the 1500, with no change of ratios. It had no synchromesh on first, and ratios were 3.67, 2.20, 1.32 and 1.00:1. An alternative close-ratio MGA gearbox was offered for racing versions. Because of the lorry-like gear-change of the MG 'box, S2 models were offered with the option of a ZF close-ratio 'box with synchromesh on all four speeds, and all Special Equipment versions (including the Super 95, 100 and 105) were fitted with this as standard. Today, the ZF's light and precise change makes it much more sought after, even though the combination of its tall first gear and the engine's poor low-down torque makes standing starts very sluggish. Ratios of 2.53, 1.71, 1.23 and 1.1:1 mean that ZF equipped Elites are particularly pleasurable in fast driving.

An 8in single dry-plate clutch from the MGA was fitted for both gearboxes, and the Hardy Spicer propshaft was used through-out. The final drive, a BMC A series differential in a Lotus alloy casing, was offered with a bewildering variety of ratios from 3.77 right up to 5.4:1 for the extremes of competition. All S1 cars for road use were delivered with 4.55:1 unless any of the options were required, while S2 Special Equipment versions had a 4.22:1 as standard. As the differential is bolted through the glass-fibre on eight half-

bush rubbers, considerable noise is transmitted into the cockpit a few inches away from the occupants' ears. What with the raucous engine noise and the lack of insulation from the gearbox and propshaft, Elite motoring is not quiet...

Elite myth has it that differentials fall out, but this simply isn't true. One pre-production Elite is known to have had its differential wrench its way out of the glass-fibre, but the thickness of the material in this area is a stag-gering ¾in. Even the most powerful racing versions suffer no such problems, so there are great margins of strength for road use – as long as the differential has been tightly fitted against the rubber mountings which provide cushioning against the glass-fibre. Cheapness and availability of most MG parts mean that transmission ailments are the least of your worries on an Elite, so the usual symptoms of weak synchromesh, whining from damaged gear teeth or clonking from the differential are not reasons to reject a car. Unfortunately, there are no ZF parts or alloy differential casings.

Body and Chassis

It is not exaggerating to say that the Elite's glass-fibre monocoque is one of the all-time great triumphs of automotive engineering. Only Turner, Jensen (with the 541) and Chevrolet (with the Corvette) had previously used the glass-fibre techniques pioneered in the marine industry, but Colin Chapman and designer Peter Kirwan-Taylor took the

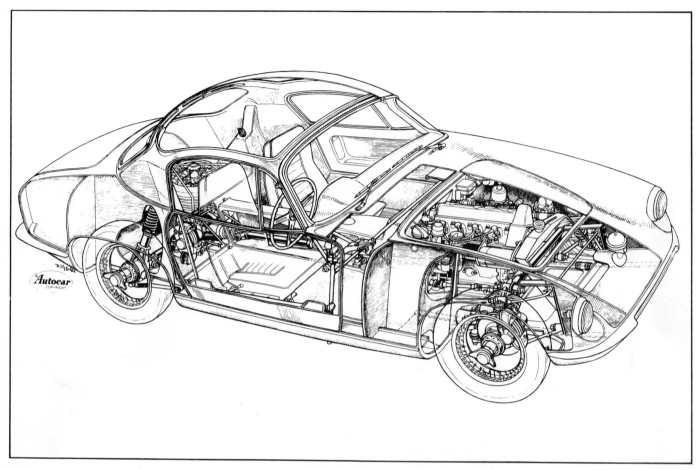

The Elite's complex glass-fibre monocoque structure can be seen clearly in this Autocar *cutaway drawing. Note the steel hoop around the windscreen and down to the sills, the Chapman strut rear suspension, the cockpit location for the spare wheel, and the all-round disc brakes (those at the rear are inboard).*

technology many steps further. To this day, the Elite is the only monocoque ever produced, although Clan made the same claim for their Crusader (and found themselves in court).

Remarkably, Kirwan-Taylor's concept remained exactly as first drawn, his combination of gorgeous flowing lines and a flat undertray producing an incredible drag coefficient of 0.29. Three decades on, the most aerodynamically conscious car makers are patting themselves on the back if they can achieve such a good figure! Needless to say, Lotus faced problems in putting this glorious idea into production. How could they create a set of moulds from a clay buck, and having made those moulds how could they fit them all together? In the end, production bodies were made from 57 different moulds, a vastly complex and expensive process which ultimately led to the adoption of a separate steel chassis for the Elan.

A total of 285 bodies for the S1 cars were made by Maximar, a Sussex-based boat building company. Despite their experience with glass-fibre, the Elite's double-skinned structure was a challenge even to their expertise, and quality suffered drastically. No two shells were quite the same in precise measurements or materials. As Maximar couldn't cope, Chapman approached the Bristol Aircraft Company with an offer of the largest glass-fibre contract ever known in Britain at the time, and their superior quality shells were used in all S2 versions. The Bristol process was slightly refined so that the number of moulds in each shell could be reduced to 43.

All mechanical components – engine, gearbox, final drive – are bolted through the glass-fibre, which was unheard of. A minimal steel subframe bonded between two skins of glass-fibre supports the front wishbone mountings, steering rack, electric fan and horns. A steel hoop bonded in around the windscreen serves as the support for the door hinges, and its base forms the jacking points. The gearbox is secured by a bolt through two metal bobbins sealed within the glass-fibre, but the differential is attached without bobbins via half rubbers either side of a conical shaped glass-fibre moulding – it really does bolt through the glass-fibre. The engine sits on a bar attached at each end through two rubber mountings directly into glass-fibre.

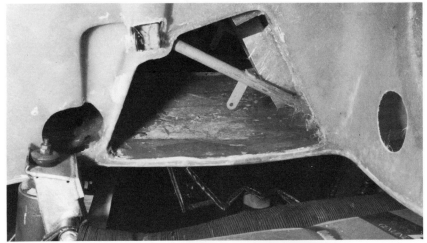

The way in which Elites are raced today with 30-year-old bodyshells is a testimonial to the amazing strength of their construction. A degree of flexing is inherent in the design, and indeed shells would break up if they were more rigid. The weight of a bare shell is only 450lb.

It is unlikely that any Elite you inspect will be free of bodywork blemishes, but all of these can be rectified. Indeed, the professional skill required to repair damaged bodies has been at such a premium over the years that many Elites have been consigned to barns through accident damage. The odd 'restoration project' Elite that crops up in the classifieds could be a good buy, but it is bound to need new bodyshell sections professionally grafted on, and a complete and labour intensive strip back to bare glass-fibre prior to repainting. All moulds exist, so it is theoretically possible to create new Elite bodyshells...

As with any glass-fibre car, all but the few really good Elites will have suffered bodily over the years from the ravages of heat, water, frost, delamination and gel-cracking. Look carefully for any bumps, dimples and hollows which indicate poor filling and re-painting where the gel has cracked. Because of the double skinned construction of the shell, all sub-surfaces – wheelarches, engine bay, boot, etc – should have a finish virtually as smooth as the exterior bodywork. 'Weetabix' surfaces of raw glass-fibre at any point

top
The boot is spacious and well-shaped, with the battery tucked neatly into the side panel. The curved intrusion is the spare wheel well.

above
A small steel subframe is bonded into the glass-fibre at the front to provide mounting points for suspension and steering. Corrosion of the exposed steel necessitates expensive and time-consuming repair work.

right
The Elite's structure seems all the more remarkable from underneath – remember that all of this flat (and aerodynamically effective) undertray is part of the glass-fibre monocoque.

except on the bulkhead inside the car are 'bodged' patching, which is as dangerous as it is undesirable. Any damage underneath the sill sections could result from incorrect jacking: it is vital to use the proper jacking point just forward of the door leading edges (at the base of the steel hoop).

Although a silver roof finish was standard on Special Equipment models, it was not compulsory, and many cars left the factory with the ordinary body colour at the request of the buyer.

There are no hidden bodyshell horrors with the Elite, but before committing yourself to a purchase it is essential to consult a professional.

Interior

Designed by Peter Cambridge, the Elite's interior is functional but not spartan. There is carpet on the floor, very comfortable vinyl high-backed Dunlop-made seats, a lightweight 16in wooden steering wheel and a full complement of instruments within a dashboard binnacle shaped rather like an Elite bodyshell in profile. Two large dials take care of speed and revs, while there are three smaller gauges for fuel, water temperature/oil pressure and battery charge. All Elites had removable plexiglass side windows which

could be stowed in pockets on the back of the seats. A heater, screen washers and seat belts were options. S2 models have stiffer Royalite thermoplastic door trim with door pockets doubling as arm rests.

Ideally an Elite should have its original trim, but such cars are rare nowadays as so few trim items can still be obtained. It is likely, therefore, that trim will be worn and cracked, or unoriginal. Some S1 cars have gained Royalite door trims, but the elbow pads could well be split and the entire surface may be ruined by extra mounting points as this trim had a tendency to pull away. Original carpets should be grey, but in many cars this has been replaced by black because it is easier to obtain. Damp carpets are not unusual because of door window leaks. The bulkhead behind the seats running up to the spare wheel housing should be covered with a ribbed grey vinyl, but again this has had to be substituted on many cars. Original carpets and vinyl in good condition are likely to be reflected by a high degree of originality and careful maintenance in the rest of the car.

No headlining should be fitted, as the authentic roof finish should be a kind of textured bird's egg dapple paint – rather like the walls of a public convenience! – which is difficult to reproduce. The instrument panel

The interior is simple and effective, but once again replacing damaged trim and instruments is a problem nowadays. Is it coincidence that the instrument panel looks like an Elite in profile?

should have a fine metallic silver/grey finish, while the dashboard binnacle is satin matt black. The Smiths instruments are unique to the Elite.

Restoration

Its technological wizardry, rarity and historical significance as Lotus's first passenger car make the Elite eminently collectable, so any degree of restoration should be cost-effective...if you can afford it.

An engine rebuild is an incredibly expensive procedure because most of the original parts are no longer available. However, the Coventry Climax in its various forms is so widely used in historic racing cars as well as in Elites that remanufacture has solved most parts problems, but at a cost. Despite the engine's heritage, there's basically nothing on the older fire pumps interchangeable with the FWE, although about two-thirds of the way through fire pump production the FWB was introduced as the basic unit. These later engines are now being discarded by fire services, and provide a good parts supply as all the castings are common to the FWE (although some machining is required). Contrary to normal practice, a Coventry Climax has to be loaded when running in, which means driving hard as the Elite is such a light car – if the piston rings aren't properly bedded in, you could end up using even more oil.

Bodyshell restoration is something you can't possibly tackle yourself. By carrying out surface preparation to a professional standard you can short-cut some labour costs, but don't even consider any glass-fibre patching as the structural integrity of an Elite depends on expert attention. The removal of existing paint to reach a bare glass-fibre surface is a painstaking business involving four or five applications of a water soluble paint stripper, then gel-cracks have to be ground out and the original glass-fibre thickness restored by fresh tissue. Filler is used to regain the precise contours before laborious rubbing down with wet and dry paper to provide a key for new paint. This is just a bare summary of the procedure – talk to the experts before you even open your can of stripper!

Although much of the interior trim was unique to the Elite, it is still available today as Miles Wilkins of Fibreglass Services and Club Elite manufactures everything. Some of the minor items were borrowed from other manufacturers: many of the switches and the door locks come from the Riley/Wolseley 1.5 range, exterior door handles from the Commer Cob van or Hillman Husky and interior handles from Triumph. Dampness in the cockpit means that seat runners have invariably rusted solid, but Triumph Herald items can be modified to fit.

Maintenance

Without scrupulous attention to maintenance schedules, no Elite is going to survive in good health for very long. While the glass-fibre chassis/body unit and proprietory transmission, suspension, steering and brake components have a very good longevity record, the engine needs regular attention.

First of all, you must not under-estimate how rapidly the Coventry Climax consumes oil. With consumption of between 150 and 300 miles a pint, it is wise to check the level after almost every journey. When Elites were new, oil was relatively cheap, but today the cost of replenishment won't be far behind your petrol bill, especially as it is easy to achieve 40mpg in an Elite. Indeed, one Elite owner told me of a friend who used to win bets by doing a 70 mile journey regularly on a gallon. Using a modern synthetic oil is pointless as you burn it up so quickly.

Because of the 'looseness' of this engine, the head needs to be tightened down every 3000 miles, with an oil and oil filter change at the same interval, even if it does seem that the rate of oil consumption amounts to a complete oil change over a shorter distance than this! The timing chain is tensioned automatically, but make sure that tappet clearances are correct. The generous clearances meant that in the engine's heyday bearing shells had to be changed every 35,000 miles.

All engine parts are available, but the cost is astronomical – a new engine will cost as much as a reasonable Elan! A fibre timing gear was fitted instead of a steel one in the FWE engine to quieten things down, but this now can't be obtained. If it strips, untold damage is done because all the valves hit the pistons, but it is likely your engine will have been fitted with the noisier steel item.

On the suspension, grease the universal joints every 500 miles. Changing a rear damper used to be a tricky job because the hub carrier into which it inserts had to be carefully heated to pull out the old damper and fit a new one, but now the inserts are just screwed in. The simple necessity of changing the rear brake pads is not difficult on S1s, but if the pad retaining pins have seized on S2s the differential has to be dropped, and to reach its securing bolts you have to remove the petrol

tank in the boot. Thankfully the Elite is so light that the brake pads – especially the rear ones – should last for years. Anyone coming to an Elite from an Elan must remember that the wire wheels tighten in the conventional direction, unlike the Elan – they should be self-tightening, not self-loosening!

Cost guidelines

Elites are far and away the most expensive Lotuses to buy. A ready market overseas – the Japanese are particularly enthusiastic – means that the best cars can fetch perhaps three times the price of a first-class Elan. It is very unlikely that any British buyer would be prepared to pay such exorbitant prices.

For the price of a running but tatty Elan you can only obtain an Elite as boxes of bits; and the price of a sound but not exceptional Elan will buy a pretty lousy running Elite. If you are in the market for an Elite, however, scarcity means that you can't be choosy. As a result, you must balance purchase price against potential restoration costs, remembering that Elite restoration on average can work out a staggering four times more costly than for the twin-cam cars. Engine rebuilds and bodywork renovation are the most expensive elements of the Elite. Interior trimming is dearer than for the Elan or Europa,

but on a par with the Plus 2.

Your course of action has to be your own judgement, but here's a thought: for the five-figure cost of restoring a 'basket case' Elite you could buy two superb Elans!

In a nutshell

Don't be misled into thinking that the Elite bears any relation to the Elan simply because it preceded it. The only link between the two cars is the name Lotus: the engine, gearboxes, final drive, brakes and construction method are completely different.

The whole question of buying an Elite must be gone into very fully, as ownership will require total commitment. If this chapter hasn't put you off, talk to Club Elite (Miles Wilkins, The Coach House, The Street, Walberton, Arundel, West Sussex) before beginning your search for a car, and do have a professional inspect and advise on any car you are thinking of buying. You wouldn't buy an old house without first having a structural survey – the same maxim applies to old cars, and none more so than the Elite.

That said, a fully restored Elite is a tremendous joy to own, with handling that is the equal of, indeed perhaps superior to, the Elan's. Properly rebuilt and maintained, an Elite should also be extremely reliable.

If you have any worries about the strength of the glass-fibre monocoque, remember that Elites are race-proven. This is a famous pair of racers: Graham Warner in LOV1 leads Les Leston in DAD10 through the Snetterton Esses in 1961.

Elan

SPECIFICATIONS	Elan S1 and S2	Elan S3
Engine	In-line four	In-line four
Construction	Cast iron block, alloy head	Cast iron block, alloy head
Bore/stroke	82.55 x 72.75mm	82.55 x 72.75mm
Capacity	1558cc	1558cc
Valves	Double ohc	Double ohc
Compression ratio	9.5:1	9.5:1
Fuel system	Twin Weber 40DCOE carburettors	Twin Weber 40DCOE carburettors
Power	105bhp at 5500rpm	105bhp at 5500rpm (115bhp at 6000rpm on Special Equipment)
Torque	108lb ft at 4000rpm	108lb ft at 4000rpm
Transmission	Four-speed manual	Four-speed manual
Final drive	3.90:1 (3.555 optional)	3.90:1 (3.777 on later cars and 3.555 optional)
Brakes	Girling discs all round (9½in front, 10in rear)	Girling discs all round (9½in front, 10in rear), servo on Special Equipment
Suspension front	Ind. by double wishbones, coil springs, telescopic dampers, anti-roll bar	Ind. by double wishbones, coil springs, telescopic dampers, anti-roll bar
Suspension rear	Ind. by Chapman strut, triangulated lower wishbones, coil springs, telescopic dampers	Ind. by Chapman strut, triangulated lower wishbones, coil springs, telescopic dampers
Steering	Rack and pinion	Rack and pinion
Wheels/tyres	Bolt-on 4½J steel wheels (knock-on optional on S2), 5.20-13 tyres (later 145 x 13 radial on S1s and all S2s)	Knock-on 4½J steel wheels, 145 x 13 tyres (155 x 13 on Special Equipment)
Body/chassis	Glass-fibre reinforced plastic body, steel box-section back bone chassis	Glass-fibre reinforced plastic body, steel box-section back-bone chassis

DIMENSIONS

	Elan S1 and S2	Elan S3
Length	12ft 1in	12ft 1in
Width	4ft 8in	4ft 8in
Height	3ft 9½in	3ft 9½in (3ft 10½in on fhc)
Wheelbase	7ft 0in	7ft 0in
Unladen weight	1410lb (S2 1485lb)	1530lb

SPECIFICATIONS

	Elan S4	Elan Sprint
Engine	In-line four	In-line four
Construction	Cast iron block, alloy head	Cast iron block, alloy head
Bore/stroke	82.55 x 72.75mm	82.55 x 72.75mm
Capacity	1558cc	1558cc
Valves	Double ohc	Double ohc
Compression ratio	9.5:1	10.3:1
Fuel system	Twin Zenith-Stromberg 175CD carburettors	Twin Weber 40DCOE or twin Dell'Orto DHLA40 carburettors
Power	105bhp at 5500rpm (118bhp at 6000rpm on Special Equipment)	126bhp at 6500rpm
Torque	108lb ft at 4000rpm	113lb ft at 5500rpm
Transmission	Four-speed manual	Four-speed manual (but five-speed manual on a few later cars)
Final drive	3.777:1 (3.555 optional)	3.777:1 (3.555 optional)
Brakes	Girling discs all round (9½in front, 10in rear, servo on Special Equipment)	Girling discs all round (9½in front, 10in rear, servo)
Suspension front	Ind. by double wishbones, coil springs, telescopic dampers, anti-roll bar	Ind. by double wishbones, coil springs, telescopic dampers, anti-roll bar
Suspension rear	Ind. by Chapman strut, triangulated lower wishbones, coil springs, telescopic dampers	Ind. by Chapman strut, triangulated lower wishbones, coil springs, telescopic dampers
Steering	Rack and pinion	Rack and pinion
Wheels/tyres	Knock-on 4½J steel wheels, 155 x 13 tyres	Knock-on 4½J steel wheels, 155 x 13 tyres
Body/chassis	Glass-fibre reinforced plastic body, steel box-section backbone chassis	Glass-fibre reinforced plastic body, steel box-section backbone chassis

DIMENSIONS

Length	12ft 1in	12ft 1in
Width	4ft 8in	4ft 8in
Height	3ft 9½in (3ft 10½in on fhc)	3ft 9½in (3ft 10½in on fhc)
Wheelbase	7ft 0in	7ft 0in
Unladen weight	1540lb	1540lb

Launched at Earls Court in 1962, the Lotus Elan was a fundamental departure from the Elite, which had been complicated and expensive to manufacture. In place of the Elite's glass-fibre monocoque came a separate steel backbone chassis, on to which was bolted a one-piece glass-fibre body. This design principle, to which Lotus has remained faithful to this day, not only reduced manufacturing costs, but also gave the Elan the great rigidity which in part accounts for its superb road manners. There was also a new engine,

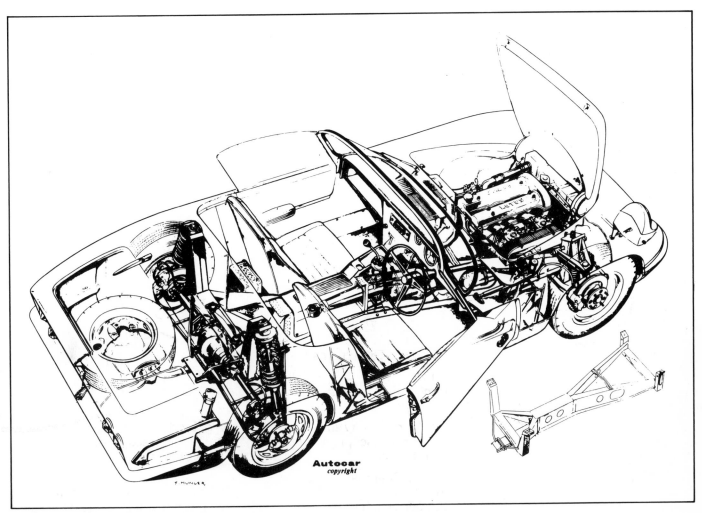

Autocar
copyright

a powerful Ford-based twin-cam producing 126bhp in the big-valve specification found in the Sprint.

Over 11 years up to 1973, a total of 12,224 Elans of all types were produced, making this by far the most prolific Lotus, as well as the one most revered by enthusiasts. Few of today's cars, designed a whole generation later, can match the handling and roadholding of a pampered Elan, and performance is still remarkable by current standards. There never has been and probably never will be anything on the road offering quite such an exquisite driving experience, and the best news for potential buyers is that Elan ownership holds no major maintenance or restoration worries.

Engine

The basis of the Elan's twin-cam engine is the five-bearing 116E Ford Cortina block, on to which is bolted a light alloy cylinder head designed by Harry Mundy. At the front of the

engine, a single roller chain drives the pair of overhead camshafts, each sitting in five bearings, and also passes over the sprocket of the redundant side camshaft on the Ford block. While its cams operate nothing, this extra camshaft is retained to drive the mechanical fuel pump, distributor and oil pump. A jockey sprocket with external adjustment maintains the timing chain's tension.

Two valves per cylinder sit in hemispherical combustion chambers, angled at 27° to the vertical and operating in replaceable cast iron guides and seats. Bucket-type tappets shroud the double valve springs, and valve clearance is set by shims of varying thickness, replacement of which requires camshaft removal. The tappets on early engines ran directly in the aluminium, but the abrasive action of dirt trapped in this soft metal soon necessitated the insertion (from engine number LP1576) of cast iron sleeves.

The cast iron crankshaft (a Lotus item) runs in five main bearings, connecting rods are of H-section in steel (at first made by Lotus, but later of Ford manufacture), and

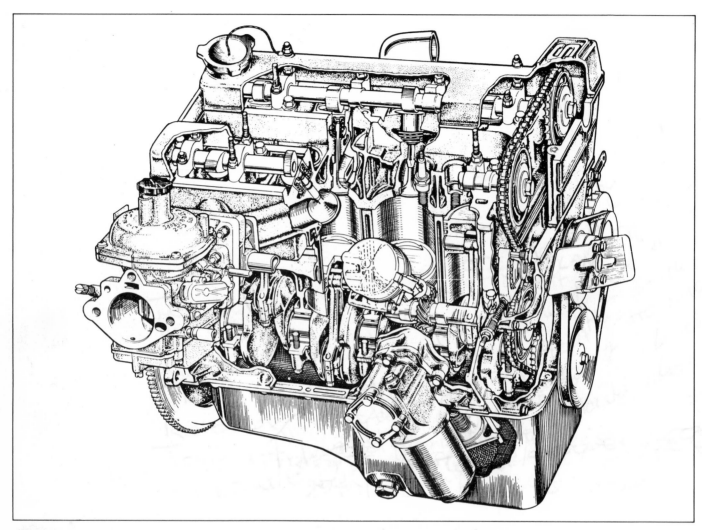

the solid-skirt pistons carry two compression rings and one oil control ring. The water pump housing is integral with the timing chain cover. All Elans have a dynamo driven by the fan belt, but there was a change from positive to negative earth from chassis number 7894.

Most Elans have a pair of Weber 40DCOE carburettors, and it was with this fuel system that the S1 appeared, producing 105bhp at 5500rpm. This is a spectacular output from just 1558cc, but more was to come! The first boost arrived with the Special Equipment specification, found on a few S2 convertibles but far more common on S3s and S4s. Power rose to 115bhp at 6000rpm thanks to the installation of a higher lift C camshaft, in place of the standard B shaft, and a new cast iron exhaust manifold with a double downpipe.

After first being tried on USA market Elans, twin Zenith-Stromberg carburettors were introduced on the S4 in November 1968 mated to cylinder heads with siamesed inlet ports. Power remained 105bhp in standard form but increased to 118bhp on Special

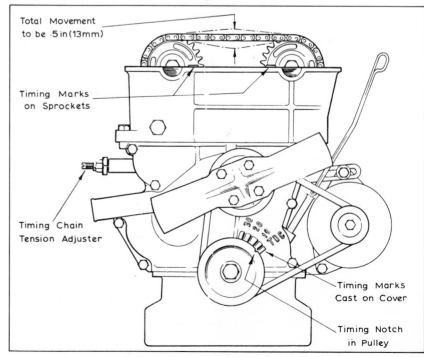

Total Movement to be .5in(13mm)

Timing Marks on Sprockets

Timing Chain Tension Adjuster

Timing Marks Cast on Cover

Timing Notch in Pulley

above
Most twin-cams have two Weber 40DCOE carburettors, but there were production phases when Dell'Ortos and Strombergs were also used.

top left
Cutaway drawing from the Elan workshop manual shows the classic Ford-based Lotus twin-cam engine. The double overhead camshaft layout driven by a long roller chain is clearly seen, and the redundant camshaft – which drives the fuel pump, oil pump and distributor – is visible alongside the block.

Workshop manual sketch view from the front of the twin-cam shows timing chain tension adjustor, correct degree of tension, and the timing notch of the water pump pulley.

Equipment cars, which were fitted with the D camshaft later found in the Sprint. Stromberg equipped cars are not the inferior machines that they are generally thought to be, but at the time the move was sufficiently unpopular with customers for Lotus to revert to Webers in October 1970.

The pride of the Elan range, the Sprint, arrived in October 1970 fitted with Tony Rudd's big-valve engine, good for 126bhp at 6500rpm. Compression ratio was raised from the standard 9.5:1 to 10.3:1, the inlet valves were enlarged (to 1.6in) and the D camshaft was fitted The Sprint was equipped with the two fabricated tubular exhaust manifolds that had been fitted to later Special Equipment cars in place of cast iron units.

The twin-cam is inherently a very reliable engine provided that it has been correctly maintained to all the schedules. Once the engine is warm, your first check should be that the oil pressure is up to the mark, which should be 38psi at 3000rpm or above. Some engines have been fitted with a high capacity oil pump, but this does more harm than good. On your test drive, listen out for any unto-

ward noises, rattles or squeaks. If the exhaust pours out blue smoke on acceleration, the piston rings have had it, and the engine is likely to need a rebore and bottom-end rebuild. If there is a puff of oil smoke on deceleration, the probable cause is worn valve guides – the clearance between guide and valve stem is fairly critical on the twin-cam. When the car is started the engine will invariably puff out a little bit of smoke, but this is nothing to worry about because the nature of the drainage tubes causes oil to sit on number four exhaust valve.

The condition of the timing chain is critical, and it must be adjusted every 3000 miles. If it is too loose you will hear it rattling, and in severe cases it can be heard swinging into the cam cover. If it is too tight it can be heard screeching. If you find the adjuster (on the inlet side of the engine) screwed fully home, it is time for a new chain. Alternatively, the attempt to take up slack could be due to the head having been skimmed so much that it is effectively useless: if this is the case, all you can do is relieve the combustion chambers to help compression or machine the tops of the piston crowns. Valve tappet noise could be caused by poor adjustment or wear: correct clearance is crucial, but worn tappets and their sleeves will need to be replaced. The water pump, contrary to popular belief, gives no trouble as long as the vee-belt, which also drives the dynamo (no Elan was ever fitted with an alternator), is not too tight. Water pump failure is invariably caused by a taut fan belt imparting excessive lateral loads. Some cars have alternative water pumps, but this is not a desirable feature.

As with all engines containing aluminium, it is essential that the cooling system contains anti-freeze, because of its corrosion inhibiting qualities, regardless of the time of year. Any signs of the ignition timing being awry are likely to be caused by a tired distributor, but new replacements are available. Lumpiness on your test drive will probably be caused by corrosion within the carburettors, which then become difficult to tune. New Webers and Dell'Ortos are availalbe. Both of these makes of carburettor are intended to sit flexibly to prevent fuel frothing in the float chambers, but plenty of over-zealous owners tighten them up excessively, thinking they are loose. This is a sure sign of ill informed owner-maintenance, suggesting that you should regard the engine with suspicion. Unless you know what you are doing, twiddling with the balance and mixture on Webers or Dell'Ortos is not a good idea.

While on the subject of carburettors, if the car you are inspecting has Strombergs bear in mind that these are prone to icing up when the temperature is one or two degrees above freezing point. In extreme cases, the throttle can be held open by ice, and there is nothing to do except stop and try to get some warmth to the carburettors. There is nothing untoward if this happens, because the factory's attempt to duct warm air round from the exhaust side didn't cure the problem. Strombergs give little trouble apart from air leakage through the spindles, indicated by overheating, pinking and running on. These carburettors should be overhauled every 12 months, but this, needless to say, is often neglected. A peculiar characteristic of Strombergs is that they cause a car to run five degrees hotter, so don't worry if the water temperature gauge is hovering around 95° on your test run.

A healthy twin-cam should never leak oil, so be wary if there's any fresh oil at the bottom of the engine or around the cam cover. S1 and S2 cars, with a four-bolt crankshaft, had a rope seal between sump and block, and this won't last beyond 15,000 miles before

starting to weep oil. Later cars with a six-bolt crankshaft had a rubber lip seal which really is oil-tight. If there are severe knocking sounds from the engine bay when it is running, check that the engine mountings have not split, leaving the engine resting on the chassis. Running temperature should be around 90° (apart from the Stromberg peculiarity already mentioned), and any overheating will be due either to a radiator blockage or to a blown head gasket – the latter will make itself very apparent when boiling point is reached!

Some Elans have been fitted with a 1600cc Ford block, indicated by a ½in aluminium spacer to retain the height between the timing cover and the head. A car with this mechanical short cut – original blocks are no longer available, but can be re-sleeved – is not to be recommended, as it's sensible to keep the twin-cam engine standard.

Suspension, steering and brakes

The all-independent suspension on the Elan is very simple, and effective. The front suspension is basically derived from the Triumph Herald, with unequal length wishbones of Lotus manufacture supporting an upright – which differed according to whether bolt-on or knock-on steel wheels were fitted – with a ball joint at the top and a trunnion below. There is an anti-roll bar running rearwards from the bottom of each of the integral Armstrong telescopic damper and spring units. The Herald steering rack is modified with a lock stop to give an increased turning circle, as the Herald's 28ft circle would physically turn an Elan over at speed. The steering column also comes from the Herald.

At the rear, suspension largely follows the Chapman strut principle seen on the Elite, except that a large wishbone instead of the driveshaft forms the lower suspension member. The wishbone is sufficiently wide-based for it to handle longitudinal location as well. After lessons learned from the Elite, the driveshafts carry Rotoflex rubber doughnut universal joints to protect the differential from road shocks. Supplied again by Armstrong, the damper/spring units which form the struts are attached at the top by Lotocone mountings on to a tower projection on the chassis, and at the bottom are shrunk into aluminium housings, each containing two thin bearings and a stub axle. Later S3 and S4 models have one thicker bearing which is much longer lasting.

Over the years, much has been written about the 'wind-up' of the Rotoflex couplings experienced with harsh throttle use, and some Elans as a result have been converted to conventional universal joint or sliding spline type couplings. The very reason for Lotus employing rubber doughnuts – to cushion the drivetrain – makes their use essential, for any car with a fixed driveshaft modification will wreck its wheel bearings very quickly and put more strain on the differential.

Start your examination of the suspension with the usual 'bounce' test to check the condition of springs and dampers – the car should rebound just once. Spring/damper units can, of course, be replaced, and it is pointless to tolerate tired dampers as the Elan's handling finesse is then lost. Left too long, the front springs can even become coil-bound. Dampers should ideally be changed every three or four years even if they don't leak in order to preserve the car's tremendous handling. Irregular tyre wear is a symptom of suspension or steering disorder. All the rubber in the suspension – bushes, Lotocone mountings and Rotoflex couplings – should be in good condition. If the car's engine does leak oil, the anti-roll bar bushes will be particularly prone to perishing. The health of the Lotocones is crucial, because after about four years they start to break up, possibly with nasty repercussions for the rear suspension and chassis.

While on the rear suspension, it is essential to check that the wheel hub flanges are true, and that the driveshaft passing through the hub carrier is also true. As the driveshaft locates on to the back face of the brake disc, any distortion will cause severe brake judder, which will be felt on your road test.

So that the Elan stops as well as it goes, all four brakes are discs, the front ones of Herald origin but the rears specially made – very few cars of the time had rear discs. The rear calipers incorporate a handbrake mechanism, consisting of a mechanical linkage with a special pair of pads, one each side of the disc. Servo assistance was included in the Special Equipment and Sprint specifications, but plenty of buyers of standard cars took up the option. The brakes are not a problem area, but make sure that the car stops smartly and in a straight line. Any shortcoming is likely to be caused by sticking pistons, which will require overhaul of the calipers. Severe judder or fade – although you would be an uncompromising buyer to induce the latter! – could also be caused by incorrect pads being used, as servo cars

The twin-cam engine in 126bhp big-valve guise. Arrows indicate the water pump and the correct state of the timing chain tensioner – a good quarter-inch of the bolt should be protruding beyond the nut.

A sure sign of inadequate maintenance attention to the twin-cam engine is the appearance of the timing chain tensioner. Almost none of the threaded bolt on the side of the timing cover is visible, meaning that timing chain renewal is overdue.

Although the Elan uses a Triumph Herald steering rack, you can't fit one straight off this mundane saloon. Without lock-stop modification, the front wheels can come close to the anti-roll bar — or even rub against it — on full lock.

Rotoflex driveshaft couplings should be in good order, with none of the perishing evident here. Conversions to solid driveshafts are not a good idea.

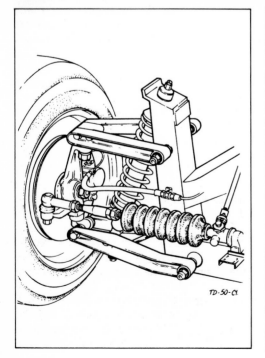

need a harder material than cars without servo. Make sure that the handbrake works well. It requires constant adjustment and is thus a good pointer to how carefully the car has been maintained.

Gearbox and rear axle

The transmission aspects of the Elan all use proprietory components, and despite being subjected to more power than in their standard applications they have proved to be fairly rugged. Although some 'running changes' were made to the gearboxes, basically two types were used: the close ratio and the semi-close ratio from the Ford Corsair 2000E, both being four-speed 'boxes. Just three Elans were built with the more troublesome Austin Maxi based five-speed 'box used in the Plus 2S 130/5, but some owners have carried out a DIY five-speed conversion, some being current Ford Sierra 'boxes. Considering that four-speed parts are readily

left
Front suspension layout of unequal-length double wishbones and coil spring/telescopic damper unit, with mounting on the chasis turret, is best seen in this sketch. The anti-roll bar is tucked below the bottom wishbone.

available, this is an unnecessary and undesirable modification which might reduce a car's value. The authentic cars have 'Sprint 5' badges.

The Ford 'boxes are delightful to use in either form. Ratios in the more sporting 'box were 2.510, 1.636, 1.230 and 1.000:1, while the semiclose ratio unit offered 2.972, 2.009, 1.396 and 1.000:1. The close ratio 'box was used on S1, S2 and some S3 Elans, while the 2000E 'box was fitted to all S4s and Sprints.

Very little goes wrong with these 'boxes apart from the usual wear and tear which results in the synchromesh rings becoming worn, a problem which will be apparent on your road test. A very loud graunching noise will probably mean that a bearing has broken up, and a complete gearbox rebuild will be necessary. This need not be a reason to reject a car as gearbox overhaul is relatively inexpensive. Before condemning a car for its gearbox noise, check whether the rubber gear lever gaiter is split — it's amazing how much noise can be transmitted through an open hole, especially as the gearbox sits directly below the lever, with no remote control linkage. The commonest area for substantial oil leakage from the gearbox is at the core plug where the propshaft enters. If this is missing, the oil shoots out all over the chassis. The four-speed change is a very precise 'click-click'. The clutch, a standard hydraulically operated Borg and Beck component, seldom gives problems.

The hypoid crownwheel and pinion is also a Ford unit (from the Anglia 105E), but with a Lotus aluminium casing. It is suspended from the rear crossmember on rubber mountings, and steadied at the bottom by rods running forwards to the bottom of the chassis. It was available with 3.9 (on S1s and earlier S2s), 3.77 (later S2s onwards) and 3.55:1 ratios (standard on S3 and S4 Special Equipment models, optional on all others). A modification found on the Sprint is a bracing bar across the lugs to spread the stresses caused by the extra power.

It is inevitable on an old car that there will be some backlash in the differential, so it is important to assess whether there is any serious wear beyond the gentle whine that is normal on a 50-60,000 mile car. At about 70mph on your test run, see if there is a loud hum when you accelerate hard or lift off. If there is, you will need either an exchange differential unit or professional setting-up of the crownwheel and pinion. The latter is not a DIY job because special tools are needed to set the shims correctly. One other possible reason for excessive noise and vibration could be that the differential is touching the chassis, which should be easily rectifiable by means of washers on the mounting bolts. Oil could be leaking from any of the oil seals, but these are cheap items to replace once the differential is out. To give it its due, however, the differential is a very robust unit if it hasn't been completely abused, and rarely gives any trouble.

Body and Chassis

The steel backbone chassis of the Elan is a deliciously simple design of great strength. Its shape is an elongated cross, the centre section forming the propshaft tunnel. At the front, it forks to form two arms either side of the engine and gearbox, the ends of these arms being connected by a crossmember with integral upright turrets providing anchorage for the spring/damper units. At the rear, there is a shorter fork, another crossmember and larger turrets to accommodate the Chapman strut upper mountings. The final drive is suspended below this crossmember. It is worth pointing out that the Elan's strength comes from the chassis and body combined.

Formed from pressed steel sheet of 16 and 18 gauge, the chassis has its central 11in deep rectangular girder drilled for lightness. When the Elan was in production, all chassis were red oxide painted and covered in bitumen, but many cars now have replacement chassis, produced either by the factory or by independent specialists. Factory items made after 1980 are galvanized and carry an eight-year guarantee, in line with mainstream production.

Apart from looking for obvious accident damage, the most important consideration is whether the chassis is original. If you buy a car with an original chassis, you are living on borrowed time, unless it is the exceptional car which has been religiously heated, had its drain holes regularly cleared and been frequently treated with Waxoyl or similar. The corrosion problems centre around the drain holes, which quickly become blocked by road dirt, causing condensation within.

The front turrets are the first areas to examine. In extreme cases the chassis will have rotted right through in those places where the drain holes have remained blocked for years. A car in this state is very dangerous, for when a turret gives way it will punch through the body and the wheel will lean in at a crazy angle. Use a small ballpein hammer or a screwdriver to check very carefully here,

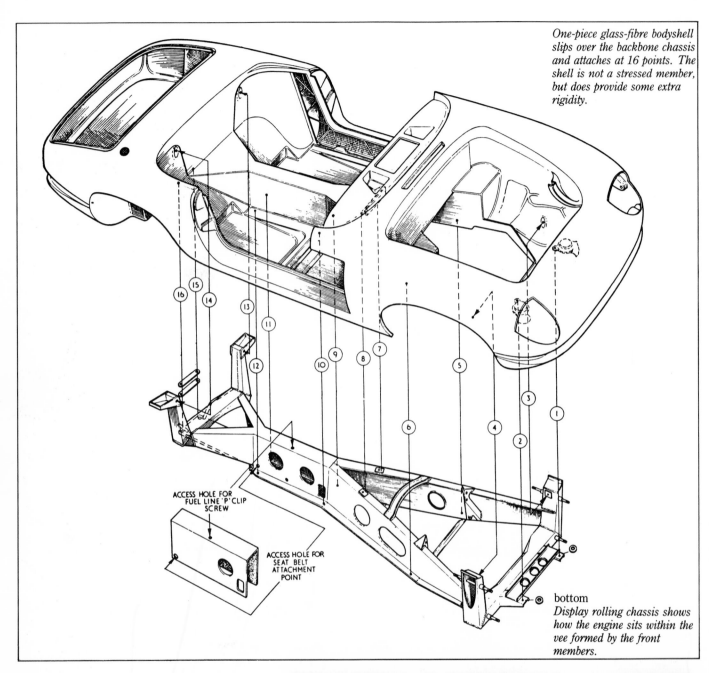

One-piece glass-fibre bodyshell slips over the backbone chassis and attaches at 16 points. The shell is not a stressed member, but does provide some extra rigidity.

ACCESS HOLE FOR
FUEL LINE 'P' CLIP
SCREW

ACCESS HOLE FOR
SEAT BELT
ATTACHMENT
POINT

bottom
Display rolling chassis shows how the engine sits within the vee formed by the front members.

and if you have any doubts the chassis must be renewed. Under no circumstances must any sheet steel be welded in because the surrounding metal will have been weakened by years of flexing. Needless to say, any evidence of such 'bodging' leads to the same conclusion: replace the chassis.

If the steering rack platform has been damaged, rack distortion can cause bump steer. It cannot physically be straightened, and a new chassis is once again the remedy. Bent fulcrum pins, cause by hitting a kerb hard, are another problem best rectified by a chassis change, although it was possible to grind out the damaged pin and weld in a new one

David Clark's fixed-head Elan Sprint is finished in the classical red and white with gold colours of Gold Leaf, Lotus's Formula 1 sponsor.

Sprints are the most desirable cars in the Elan range. Two departures from originality on this car are the 'Stromberg' bonnet bulge and normal finish, instead of black, wheel centres.

Elan interiors evolved gradually, but all had wood veneer dashboards. S4 and Sprint models had rocker switches for the minor controls in the centre.

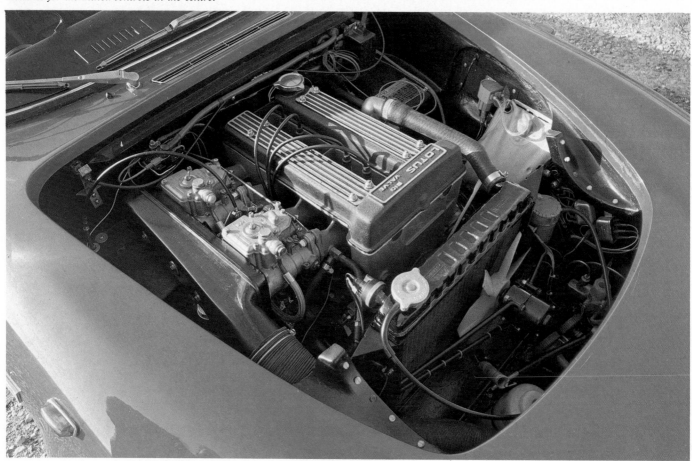

The Elan Sprint used Tony Rudd's big-valved 126bhp version of the twin-cam engine.

The steel chassis is the most vulnerable part of an Elan, and most cars by now have received a new one. Lotus-manufactured replacements in galvanised steel (with an eight-year guarantee) are cheap and relatively easily fitted, and are definitely preferable to any alternative make of chassis.

right and below right
The best guide to the state of the chassis is found by checking the base of the front turrets. The sort of corrosion evident in these two photographs is encouraged by blocked drainage holes, and would definitely require a new chassis.

when Elans were in production. Don't be misled by this into thinking that repair here is a good idea, for one is welding near the front crossmember, which carries the vacuum for the retractable lamps as well as fuel droplets – you could blow yourself up! Talking of headlamps, a hissing noise when you switch off is likely to be the result of corrosion causing a pinprick hole through the crossmember, which destroys the vacuum. Once again, it would be stupid to attempt to weld this up.

At the rear, there are normally no problems unless the car has been run on worn springs and dampers, in which case what is virtually a solid rod will have caused distortion by banging into the top of the chassis. It is also necessary to check whether there is any chassis puckering around the differential, indicating that the car has received a side impact on the rear wheel, possibly only through clobbering a kerb, which has pushed the wishbone inwards. Look also behind the engine mounting bracket to see if any cracks have been created by weight bearing down from an engine on broken mountings.

If you have any doubts whatever about the chassis, replacement is essential. Paint will not take to a galvanized chassis until it has weathered, but some owners do apply paint. All you have to do to satisfy yourself if a chassis is claimed to be new is to make a judicious scratch to see if it is galvanized.

The glass-fibre bodyshell fits over the backbone like a saddle, and is attached to it by 16 bolts. It is a hand-made single-piece unit (although it was moulded in upper and lower sections at the factory). Where the bodyshell has to receive attachment bolts,

aluminium bobbins with internal threading are bonded into the moulding. At the door sills steel frames were incorporated in the mouldings. The entire shell is extremely strong and light, weighing only 250lb in convertible form.

Elans have either convertible or fixed-head body styles, but the latter arrived only with the S3 in 1965; before that you could order a closed car by specifying the optional factory hard-top. There were changes to the bodyshell throughout the Elan's life. S1 cars had a pair of separate tail lamps on each side, but on S2s the lamps were combined in a single cluster on each side. The major body changes for the S3 were to extend the boot lid over the top of the vertical tail panel and to introduce framed door windows on the convertible. S4s were given more angular flared wheel arches to accommodate 155 width tyres. The complexity of badging is incredible, changes having been made all the time by Lotus, but one rule that can be stated is that S1-S3 cars have a script badge, while S4s and Sprints have a more fashionable block badge. Elans have glass-fibre bumpers which on all cars were foam-filled – the idea was that they would retain their shape after a knock, but it didn't work in practice. Modern replacement bumpers do not have foam filling. From the originality point of view, bumpers and wheels are a worthwhile check. Apart from the Sprint, with black wheels, all Elans had silver painted steel disc wheels. All Elans had silver painted bumpers as standard, although the factory did produce some special black bumpers for S2 and S3 cars to order. Sprints should have gold bumpers,

left
It is foolish to attempt to salvage a damaged or corroded – and therefore weakened – chassis, particularly as a replacement is not expensive, but some unscrupulous 'specialists' have been known to do this. Flat surfaces really should be flat, this ridge indicating a welded repair.

above
Here's one way to examine the chassis if you don't have an inspection hoist! This car has a Spyder replacement chassis – that circular section cross-beam at the front is an obvious clue.

top right
Another view of the Elan S1 as introduced in 1962 – the shape was startlingly modern for the time.

middle right
November 1964 brought the S2, with a host of minor changes including a full-width wooden dashboard and one-piece tail lamps. Knock-on steel wheels became an option.

bottom right
The fixed-head coupé body style came with the S3 announced in September 1965. This Elan has the chromed bumpers which were fitted to a few press and demonstrator cars.

and no Elan apart from the Mike Spence BRM cars of 1967-68 ever had dayglow orange bumpers.

No Elan bodies were ever self-coloured, paint being of the cellulose type except for the polyurethane painted later Sprints. The bodyshell gives very little trouble in service apart from the usual glass-fibre trait of gel-cracking at major stress points. Look for cracks around the door handles, boot lock, fuel filler and where the bonnet is pushed down. Like any other glass-fibre car, the Elan's bodyshell can physically move more than a metal body, so it is essential to check that doors, bonnet and boot fit correctly. In extreme cases, the doors can drop dramatically when they are opened, and this will mean that the hinges will have to be re-aligned.

You will be very lucky to find a car with an unblemished original body, but if you do, buy the car regardless of the rest of its condition! There are plenty of cars still wearing the original cellulose paint, but natural weathering will have taken its course and the paint will be faded and almost certainly covered in micro-blisters. This is common, and really leaves no alternative to taking the car back to bare glass-fibre and starting again.

Very careful examination of the entire body is essential, as sub-standard resprays are sadly very common. To achieve a cheap tart-up, too many people blow paint over gel-cracks and wodges of filler. Hollows, rings and sandpaper marks under the surface will all indicate a 'bodged' job which might as well not have been done at all. A rub-down and repaint in such instances could just exaggerate the eyesore, so bear in mind that a glass-fibre respray is a labour-intensive and costly job when weighing up the bodywork.

Look also for accident damage. Any inadequate work will be obvious, but the more cleverly disguised repairs need to be sought out. Run your fingers under the front and rear wheelarches to see if new sections have been bonded on, and lift up the carpet and felt to make sure this beautiful Elan is not two cars literally stitched together. If there are signs of joints, ask the owner for evidence of who carried out the repair work, since a recognized professional's work does not detract from the car's value. Poor quality repair raises question marks about safety as well as value.

If you're buying an Elan with restoration in mind, be wary of possible frost damage to a car which has been sitting outside for years gathering condensation under a plastic sheet. A respray on a shell containing water drop-

right
You should pay very careful attention to the bodywork, even if a car is claimed to have had a recent respray. Only the very best restored cars will be free of any gel cracking, and the only way to cure the problem is to rub back to bare glass-fibre before painting.

far right
Proper bodywork restoration requires that gel cracks should be ground out and repaired with fresh glass-fibre tissue followed by a coating of resin.

right
All sorts of inadequate repairs can lie below relatively innocuous surface blemishes. This bonnet panel has had its bulge (for Stromberg carburettors) removed and the hole crudely filled. The gouge shows a quarter-inch of filler.

far right
Bare glass-fibre — the dark patches on this Elan wing — has a slightly translucent appearance. The pale areas are filler where someone has attempted literally to cover up blemishes. The gouges (arrowed) will have to be ground out and repaired with tissue and resin.

right
Elan half way through the long process of preparation before painting.

above left
The S3 convertible came later than the fixed-head, in June 1966. Framed door windows to go with electric operation are the most obvious change, but the revised hood fitting and larger boot lid (a feature of all S3 and subsequent Elans) extending over the tail panel can be seen clearly.

bottom left
The S4 — shown in fixed-head Sprint guise giving its Rotoflex driveshaft couplings some stick on a standing start! — brought more minor body changes, including larger tail lamps and squared-off wheel arches with greater flaring.

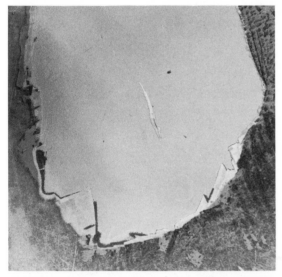

lets will cause the paint to blister, and severe frost damage could affect the safety of the car.

Interior

Although the original Elan has a very stark cockpit compared with later versions, it is as comfortable and functional as it needs to be, fitting the driver like the proverbial glove. You sit snugly between the door and high transmission tunnel, your legs stretching out ahead in the roomy footwell, where pedal positions are ideally arranged for heel and toe operation.

The S1's oiled teak dashboard housed a lidless glovebox and black bezelled instruments, comprising speedometer, tachometer, fuel gauge and combined oil pressure/water temperature gauge. Rubber mats covered the floor and the fore/aft adjustable seats were trimmed in black vinyl. Windows had simple push-up operation, but at least this allowed sufficient hollow in the doors to make a convenient armrest. The steering wheel was at first a cheap wooden affair (but later became leather-rimmed up to the S4, and vinyl-rimmed for the Sprint), an umbrella handbrake was placed under the right hand side of the dashboard, and a heater was standard. Switches were neatly placed, and two column stalks took care of indicating and dipping. The hood was extremely crude, with stays separate from the fabric – a nightmare in a sudden shower!

From these basic beginnings, the interior specification improved gradually. The S2 gained a proper varnished dashboard with a lockable glovebox (although later S1s had a makeshift glovebox lid), interior door handles and door trim were altered, pedal pads became smaller and the switch layout was mildly revised.

More substantial cockpit changes came with the S3. Frames for the door windows stopped the old winter bugbear of the glasses bowing and letting in a draught, and electrically-operated windows provided a touch of gadget appeal. The dashboard gained a plastic lip along its lower edge, and the switch layout was revised again. The battery moved from behind the seats to the boot. A much neater hood was fitted, this one folding conventionally into a tray behind the passenger compartment.

For the S4, small concessions to modernity were made. Fresh air vents appeared on each end of the dashboard, rocker switches replaced the old toggles, and MGB flush door handles (used by Lotus well into the eight-

ies!) were fitted in new ventilated plastic door trims, this fabric matching new seat coverings. Instrument lettering became a heavier block type. A steering lock replaced the Elan's traditional key start on the Sprints.

When inspecting the interior of an S1 and S2, make sure that all the trim is in place and undamaged, as all trim items now have to be remade by hand. In view of this, carpet in place of the rubber mats is an acceptable departure from originality. Broken manual window mechanisms on these early cars have to be re-made but guide channels, door seals and rubbers are still obtainable. At no time were Elans ever trimmed with leather or cloth, so avoid a car which lacks the original vinyl unless you are prepared to have a specialist trimmer carry out the replacement.

There are fewer parts problems for S3, S4 and Sprint interiors, but originality and completeness of trim are still important. It's remarkable how many cars have been spoiled by holes cut for extra instruments, stereo units and loudspeakers. New dashboards of both types are available, but installation is time-consuming. Bear in mind, if the dashboard is scratched, that the veneer is so thin on its marine ply backing that rubbing back will destroy it. Torn headlinings can easily be replaced.

In short, a sound interior is a considerable advantage, but you ought not dismiss a car because of interior shortcomings – instead use them as bargaining points.

Restoration

Unlike so many lesser cars, Elan restoration is usually cost-effective and relatively simple. No car, no matter how decayed, is beyond redemption, from either cost or parts points of view. Naturally, it makes sense to buy the best car you can afford, but avoid the temptation to buy a car in the middle price bracket, which in the long run could cost just as much as a non-runner.

Apart from the obvious areas – bodywork, engine, gearbox, etc – best left to a specialist, Elans are reasonably straightforward for the home restorer to handle. There are plenty of books available, a workshop manual is invaluable, and there is always professional advice available at the end of a telephone. Professional help, of course, costs money, but Elans are 120mph cars on which safe steering, suspension and brakes are vital. Even if you get stuck in your restoration and a professional has to finish the job for you, at the end of the day you should still have a car worth substantially more than you paid for it.

The S1's cockpit was neat, but starkly trimmed compared with later Elans. The dashboard has wood veneer, the passenger's cubby hole has no lid, and this style of wooden-rimmed steering wheel is unique to S1s. The crude cable door pull is just visible on the right.

S3 facias differed from those of S2s in several ways, the lower edge now having a padded finish and the ashtray being set into the dashboard in the centre. This car has the earlier style leather-rimmed steering wheel — later S3s had perforated spokes.

S4 interior changes were substantial: rocker switches now take care of minor controls, seat facings have perforated vinyl, smarter door trim includes recessed handles, and ventilation flaps appear at each end of the facia.

On the engine side, every single part except for the block itself is available, so overhauls, though not cheap, present no real difficulties. There is no excuse for not keeping your twin-cam utterly standard! There are many twin-cam specialists, but as the reputation of some is not whiter than white it is wise to ask around among Elan owning acquaintances.

The twin-cam block can only be bored out to 40 thou, not to the 60 thou that is possible with standard Ford blocks. Once you are at the 40 thou, the block does not become useless as it can be re-sleeved and returned to standard. This is common practice, and although it is an expensive procedure it does mean that your twin-cam block can go on forever. There are no worries about the availability of new crankshafts, connecting rods or pistons. All head problems – oversize guides or seats, for example – can be rectified. Parts prices are not excessive, but the fact that a complete strip and rebuild takes 40-45 hours will come into the cost reckonings. Main and big end bearings must be Lotus components, as the Ford components, which do fit, will knock out within 5000 miles.

Gearbox overhaul is one of the easiest aspects of Elan restoration, but a split final drive casing could be a problem as new ones are not available. You will have to search for a firm that can carry out aluminium welding in order to salvage a damaged casing.

Sooner or later, a car with an original chassis will need a replacement unit, and it is strongly advisable to buy a factory item even though alternatives – notably the Spyder chassis – are available. Compared with the original production chassis, new ones have been strengthened up with extra flitch plates at the weak points. All genuine works replacements carry an LR number (for Lotus Replacement).

If a chassis is bent, you will be deluding yourself if you attempt to pull it out with chain equipment. Welding new sections on to old, fatigued steel is most unwise, and the workshop manual emphasizes this. A new chassis is so cheap that it's foolish even to consider such short cuts. If you have to embark on a chassis change, it makes a great deal of sense to carry out all restoration work in one go – try to fit as much new running gear as you can afford, replacing all brakes, suspension, bushes and so on. By doing this you will then have at least five or six years of trouble-free motoring. If you can't afford to do this, you will be forever chasing your tail and your Elan will become a drudge, not a joy.

While chassis replacement is inexpensive, bodywork restoration on an Elan is quite costly because preparing glass-fibre before repainting takes so long. Cutting out damaged sections and bonding in new ones is likely to be a job for professionals, but you can probably handle the surface preparation yourself. It is sensible to strip the car back to bare glass-fibre if it has already had two or more resprays because invisible blemishes will show up when the new coat is applied, as the thinners in paint will soften up the previous layers. Use only Nitromors water soluble stripper as anything containing a stronger alkali will attack the glass-fibre.

All of the subtly different Elan bodyshells, door, bonnet and boot lid panels, headlamp pods and bumpers are available from the factory. It may well be easier to buy a new bonnet, for example, rather than spend hours trying to scrape everything off an old one.

Elan owners are lucky in having so many replacement parts available from the factory. It is usually cheaper to graft on a new body section — this is a front corner — rather than attempt to repair accident damage.

Maintenance

As with any other classic cars, Elans were generally bought in the first place by discerning people who followed the maintenance schedules to the letter, but later in life they sometimes passed on to owners who either didn't bother with regular maintenance or couldn't afford it. Thankfully, Elans have always been so desirable that ill-maintained examples are not the norm. You should, of course, follow the maintenance schedules as much for safety reasons as to protect the value of your car, and with proper attention an Elan is very reliable.

There are plenty of classic car owners who believe in using their cars very infrequently, on the occasional summer day. This is more unkind to the car than doing around 4000 miles a year because any make of car has to be used to avoid regular overhauling of the brakes, changing of the water pump and so on.

Oil and oil filter should be changed and timing chain tension examined every 3000 miles, while every 6000 miles tappets need to be checked and adjusted, and plugs and points renewed. Air filters should be changed at 12,000 miles. Keep anti-freeze in the engine all the year round. As long as it has been properly rebuilt and maintained, a twin-cam engine should last at least 80,000 miles, and some have done over 120,000 – it is a very strong unit. A healthy engine should use oil at the rate of a pint every 450 miles.

Properly looked after, the water pump need not be the problem that twin-cam myth has made it. It should be assembled from the genuine Lotus kits, and the fan belt should not be too taut. Infrequent use is often the reason for failure, and if this happens it will take a whole weekend to fit a new one because the sump and head have to be removed to reach the front cover which houses the water pump.

Suspension maintenance is relatively simple, but essential to preserve the Elan's handling. Dampers should be changed every three or four years even if they appear to be sound, and regular maintenance consists of greasing the swivels at the front every 3000 miles, and the steering rack's grease nipple every 12,000 miles. The rear suspension needs no regular maintenance whatsoever, although if carrying out fitting yourself make sure that the wishbone bolts are lubricated so that you can withdraw them at a later date. For safety's sake, it is a good idea to change

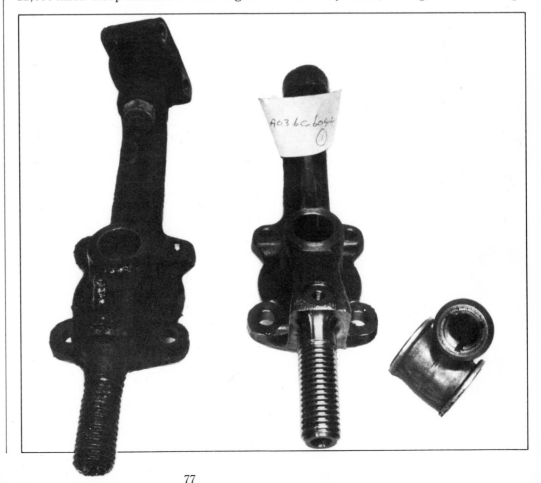

This comparison between a new front upright and a badly worn example shows the damage that could be hidden within the brass trunnion. The thread has become worn because of infrequent lubrication.

the trunnion kit – the little plastic bush containing a steel sleeve through which the trunnion bolt passes – every 10,000 miles. If wear is allowed to advance, the brass trunnion and even the entire bottom wishbone can be destroyed.

The brakes are unlikely to cause trouble in service as long as all the seals on the calipers are replaced every three years. Rusty or corroded pistons should naturally be replaced. If you use the car regularly in bad weather, the rear brake pads will probably need replacing as often as every 3000 miles because of the road dirt that becomes trapped between disc and pad owing to the exposed position on the inboard side of the hub carrier. Front pads, on the other hand, can last more than 30,000 miles if you don't drive too enthusiastically. When replacing a servo, it's vital to obtain an Elan unit with 2:1 boost – fitting the Plus 2 3:1 unit in an Elan will cause you to stop more dramatically than you intend. Unfortunately, the original Girling servos and their overhaul kits are no longer available, but there is a suitable Lockheed equivalent. Although it's rarely done, brake hoses and seals should be changed every three years. On a car used infrequently, silicon brake fluid is preferable to the conventional fluid because it doesn't absorb water.

Ford gearboxes are hardy units if kept properly supplied with new EP80 oil every 6000 miles and checked every 3000, while the differential requires EP90 which should be changed every 12,000 miles and checked every 3000 – confusing these two oils is asking for trouble. Any leaks from gearbox or differential are caused by infrequent replacement of oil seals. Oil from the differential can leak through the pinion oil seal, through the side seals around the output shafts or through the nose piece. The gearbox will leak through the front or rear oil seals. In any of these instances, it is worth the expense of a few pounds to replace these seals whenever the gearbox or differential is taken out.

Whether or not your Elan has a new chassis, it is vital that you keep the drain-holes religiously cleared to prevent internal corrosion. On the original production chassis, there was only one drain hole on each side of the front turrets, but it is prudent to enlarge them to around ½in in diameter and make additional holes on the other side of the turrets.

Cost guidelines

All Elans are steadily appreciating in value. There is little difference in prices between the models, with the exception of the Sprint which carries a premium of about 15 per cent. The relative rarity nowadays of the S1 is balanced by its less desirable specification. Special Equipment models were worth a little more. As so few Elans nowadays are used as daily transport, the practicality of the fixed-head is not as important to buyers, so expect a convertible body to have a small influence on pricing.

With a good few thousand Elans in reasonable running order in Britain, prices are mercifully not in the same league as the rare Elite, for which demand from abroad has caused dramatic price inflation. A later Elan is likely to cost a third to a half as much again as a twin-cam Europa. The worst 'basket case' Elans are still very cheap, and an excellent buy if you are competent to carry out most of the restoration yourself. The best cars, on the other hand, are in demand and could cost the same as a typical modern family saloon. As advised earlier, think very carefully about the degree of restoration work required on a car in the middle price ranges, as it could turn out to be nearly as expensive as restoring a much cheaper car.

In a nutshell

Ownership of a mechanically and structurally sound Elan will be a great joy when you come to appreciate the blistering performance and superb handling which make these cars so sought after. While restoration presents no special difficulties, time spent searching for the right car will definitely be repaid. After all, your Elan is unlikely to be your day-to-day car, so there is no excuse for rushing into a purchase that you might later regret.

When examining any car, you must constantly weigh up restoration costs against the purchase price. The more cars you can look at to get a feel for the market, the better. Unless your knowledge is very extensive, when you have satisfied yourself that you have found a good car, seek professional help before you part with any money. Any Lotus Classic Dealer – at the time of writing there are eight in this scheme dedicated solely to promoting the twin-cam era cars – will be happy to inspect the car of your choice for a modest fee. This is much better than taking your friend who knows all about them, because the chances are that he doesn't. Some specialists are better than others, and word of mouth recommendation from club members is the way to find the best ones.

Plus 2

SPECIFICATIONS	Plus 2 and Plus 2S	Plus 2S 130
Engine	In-line four	In-line four
Construction	Cast iron block, alloy head	Cast iron block, alloy head
Bore/stroke	82.55 x 72.75mm	82.55 x 72.75mm
Capacity	1558cc	1558cc
Valves	Double ohc	Double ohc
Compression ratio	9.5:1	10.3:1
Fuel system	Twin Weber 40DCOE carburettors (twin Zenith-Stromberg 175Cd on Plus 2	Twin Weber 40DCOE carburettors
Power	115bhp at 6250rpm	126bhp at 6500rpm
Torque	108lb ft at 4000rpm	113lb ft at 5500rpm
Transmission	Four-speed manual	Four-speed manual (but five-speed manual on Plus 2S 130/5)
Final drive	3.777:1	3.777:1
Brakes	Girling discs all round (10in front, and rear, servo)	Girling discs all round (10in front and rear, servo)
Suspension front	Ind. by double wishbones, coil springs, telescopic dampers, anti-roll bar	Ind. by double wishbones, coil springs, telescopic dampers, anti-roll bar
Suspension rear	Ind. by Chapman strut, fixed length driveshafts, triangulated lower wishbones, coil springs, telescopic dampers	Ind. by Chapman strut, fixed length driveshafts, triangulated lower wishbones, coil springs, telescopic dampers
Steering	Rack and pinion	Rack and pinion
Wheels/tyres	Knock-on 5½J steel wheels, 165 x 13 tyres	Knock-on 5½J steel wheels, 165 x 13 tyres
Body/chassis	Glass-fibre reinforced plastic body, steel box-section back-bone chassis	Glass-fibre reinforced plastic body, steel box-section back-bone chassis

DIMENSIONS

Length	14ft 0in	14ft 0in
Width	5ft 3½in	5ft 3½in
Height	3ft 11in	3ft 11in
Wheelbase	8ft 0in	8ft 0in
Unladen weight	1880lb (Plus 2S 1970lb)	1970lb

From the potential buyer's point of view, there's nothing special about the Plus 2, for it is really only an Elan in a different bodyshell. Indeed, it was labelled the Elan +2 when it was launched, but very soon its name became abbreviated to the simple 'Plus 2'. If you're thinking of buying one of these 'family man's Elans', therefore, all the guidelines covered in the previous chapter apply with the exception of the minor specification changes introduced as the Plus 2's evolution diverged from the Elan's.

With its pair of occasional rear seats and seductive fixed-head styling, the Plus 2 is certainly an appealing car which in the end outlasted the Elan in the market-place by a year. Launched in June 1967, it was larger in every direction than the Elan, offering much more interior space. A foot was added to the wheelbase, nearly 2ft to the length and 7in to the width, giving a much more spacious interior. The twin-cam engine produced 115bhp at 6000rpm (the same tune as Special Equipment Elans) using Weber carburettors. Zenith-Stromberg carburettors were fitted to the Plus 2S to give 118bhp, but the arrival of the Plus 2S 130 saw the return of Webers (and later Dell' Ortos).

While the Ford four-speed gearbox and differential (with 3.77:1 final drive) were both retained, changes were made to suspension and drivetrain to fit the Plus 2's increased

dimensions. Wishbones, steering links, driveshafts and propshaft were all lengthened, but all the principles were identical to the Elan. The differential was the same as the Elan. A brake servo was standard (this was always part of the Special Equipment package on the Elan) and the front discs were increased by ½in to 10in diameter to cope with the weight gain. Larger calipers were used at the front.

The backbone chassis was substantially the same apart from its 12in greater length.

above
Launched in June 1967, the Elan +2 was the Lotus for the family man, its elegant styling concealing two occasional rear seats. Later the 'Elan' designation was dropped and the car became known simply as the Plus 2.

top right
The Plus 2's cockpit was more sumptuous than any Elan's. The comprehensively equipped burr walnut veneer dashboard included fresh air vents and auxiliary dials for fuel level, oil pressure, water temperature and battery charge.

middle right
Further interior improvements came with the Plus 2S in March 1969. Note the extra padding on the centre console, neat trim under the facia, a map reading light on the passenger side, new rocker switches and two extra instruments (for clock and ambient temperature).

bottom right
Oatmeal trim, as on this Plus 2S 130/5, is the most desirable of all 130 specifications, but make sure that the materials are authentic.

left
This sketch shows the body to chassis attachment points. The structural arrangement is similar to the Elan except that the bodyshell incorporates steel side members.

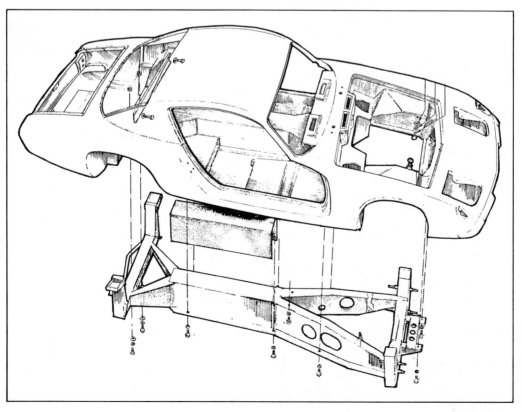

Minor changes included the rear fork in the structure being slightly widened so that the inward inclination of the Chapman struts remained the same as on the Elan. Any stiffness lost in lengthening the chassis was more than made up by a more rigid body which incorporated triangulated steel side members in the sills – these also served as seat belt mounting and jacking points. Drag coefficient increased from the Elan's 0.31 to 0.32, and chromed bumpers (the front one from the Ford Anglia, the rear made up of two halves of a Riley Elf/Wolseley Hornet item with a bit extra in the middle) appeared for the first time on a Lotus.

Like the Elan, the earliest cars had a cast iron exhaust manifold, but this was later changed to a fabricated version integral with the downpipe. Earlier cars also had a transverse silencer box at the rear, but this was soon changed to a longitudinal unit.

The interior was much more luxurious than the Elan's, in keeping with its higher price (it was only £50 cheaper than the Jaguar E-type when launched) and more middle-aged market. The front seats were fixed but tipped forwards to allow access to the rear, and the greater interior width allowed nicely padded door trims. On the burr walnut veneer dashboard were large dials for speed and revs, and four smaller ones in the centre of the facia for fuel, oil pressure, ammeter and water temperature. All had white needles and a black background. In order to maintain the Elan's roadholding standards, wider 165 x 13 tyres were fitted to knock-on steel rims.

The first major evolutionary change came with the more desirable Plus 2S introduced in March 1969. Its main improvement was a more luxurious interior, with plusher reclining seats, a padded centre console in place of the earlier model's hard plastic, recessed door handles, a map light and two extra dials for a clock and ambient air temperature. All instruments now had red needles. Fog lamps also became standard. A Herald steering column replaced the Cortina single-piece item of the earlier Plus 2. The new model was really significant, however, in being the first Lotus available only fully-built – these were early signs of Colin Chapman's desire to move gradually up-market, a trend which reached real fruition in 1973 with the introduction of the new generation Elite.

When the car received the 126bhp big-valve twin-cam in October 1970, at the same time as the Elan Sprint became available, it was given an even longer name – Plus 2S 130. To cope with the extra power, the drivetrain was strengthened: there was a differential bracing bar to spread the stresses and stiffer Rotoflex couplings. Altered headlamp mechanism meant that any loss of vacuum in the front chassis crossmember would keep the headlamps up, not down – why didn't they think of it before? Apart from the badging, many Plus 2S 130s are recognizable by their metallic silver roofs, a commonly specified factory option. On the earliest cars this was painted conventionally, but soon a self-colouring process was introduced whereby coarse aluminium flakes were laid-up in the gel coat. Cars in John Player Special colours had a gold flake in the gel coat, and this finish was applied to the sills too.

As Lotus wanted to use the Plus 2 as a test bed for the five-speed gearbox of the forthcoming new Elite, this option was announced on the Plus 2S 130/5 in October 1972. Initial acceleration on ratios of 3.20, 2.00, 1.37, 1.00 and 0.87:1 was actually a fraction slower, but the same top speed of 121mph was achieved at 1400rpm lower. Using Austin Maxi internals within a Lotus aluminium casing, this 'box always had a pretty sloppy gearchange, and isn't as desirable today as it sounds.

While four-speed gearboxes are fairly trouble-free, the five-speed is prone to whine in fifth gear because the tailshaft bearing doesn't receive its fair dose of oil, and eventually will start to run dry. If you find a car with this whine, bear in mind that the cost of dismantling the 'box and changing the bearing is high. Check the synchromesh on down-changes as an owner who has tried to hurry his changes may have damaged the synchro rings. Four-speed repair costs are generally lower, and the fuel consumption advantage of the five-speed is only apparent if you do a lot of motorway driving. It is important to listen for differential whine too, and the mounting points should be in perfect order. The Plus 2's weight means that it is specially important to check damper condition.

Almost all the advice in the Elan chapter applies to the Plus 2 range because of the mechanical and structural similarity. The chassis and bodyshell weak points are just the same. One feature not shared with the Elan are the steel members in the sills: check these for both soundness and 'bodging', for there may have been an attempt to disguise collapse at the jacking points. It is worth checking the condition of windscreen seals as there are parts problems on some models. The simple rubber surround with an infill strip on original Plus 2s can be replaced, but

Extreme cases of chassis rot can have severe results. On this Plus 2 the front turret has started to punch through the glass-fibre in the wheel arch area, the owner having made a rather pathetic attempt to hold it back with a pop-riveted metal plate.

far right
Plus 2s have extra steel strengthening members along the cockpit sills which form mud traps at their forward ends. Advanced corrosion is easily visible in this case with the nose section cut away, but you can spot it by peering under the wheelarches.

top left
Apart from its extra cockpit space, the larger luggage boot is the Plus 2's other advantage over Elans. The earliest cars have a shallower compartment, but all have this crude looking but effective supporting strut.

middle left
For most people the definitive Plus 2 is the 130 with black knock-on steel wheels and a silver roof. Bear in mind when buying that this finish is expensive to recreate if it has deteriorated.

bottom left
Exposed headlamps on a Plus 2 are a sure sign of severe chassis corrosion. A vacuum in the front cross-member should keep the pods retracted, but corrosion eventually punctures the vacuum.

on Plus 2Ss the different rubber with a wide chrome strip cannot be obtained, replacement having to be to the old pattern. Federal regulations caused all Plus 2S 130s to be fitted with bonded windscreens, which are not interchangeable with rubber sealed 'screens and are far more expensive to replace.

The metallic flake roof finish of Plus 2S 130s may sound very attractive, but make sure that it's not cracked and discoloured. Because the aluminium (or gold-coloured) flakes are in the gel coat, it's only possible to re-create this finish nowadays by use of customizing metallic candied paints. You can revert to the painted finish which came on the earliest Plus 2S 130s, but it's much better to find a car with a good original roof finish. A poor JPS roof really is a headache to restore authentically, and a metallic roof on anything other than a Plus 2S 130 is unoriginal. Wing mirrors or a sun-roof would not have been fitted by the factory, and the latter is not a good thing as some of the bodyshell's strength is lost – you are quite likely to find gel-cracks around a sun-roof. A damaged or rusty front bumper is not a real problem, but replacing the Elf/Hornet rear bumper is very expensive as a new unit has to be made.

One of the Plus 2's most appealing aspects is its plush interior, generally finished in black vinyl. As with the Europa, oatmeal trim was a late model option (with ribbed inserts on the last Plus 2S 130/5 models), and today carries a slight price premium. If you inspect a car with an oatmeal interior, do make sure that all the trim is original and undamaged. Grubbiness can largely be removed by professional valeting but replacing torn or excessively worn trim is a problem as the authentic vinyl is scare and expensive. As a result, many cars have been retrimmed with the wrong kind of oatmeal. Since originality is always important to the value of a car, it's accepting second-best to buy a Plus 2 with the wrong trim, no matter how well the work has been done – after you've seen a car with the correct oatmeal upholstery, a substitute will be obvious.

While on the subject of originality, cabriolet conversions of Plus 2s are not uncommon, around 50 believed to have been 'chopped' at the time of writing. Hexagon of Highgate made two cabriolets in the early seventies, and more recently Christopher Neil Sportscars and the Classic Transport Co have carried out their own conversions. While the Hexagon cabriolets are universally considered to have been painstakingly re-engineered to compensate for losing the rigidity of the roof section (so much so that the cost was prohibitive), these later unofficial versions have met with criticism. While the makers have strongly defended the quality of their work, the question mark about loss of structural rigidity – causing inferior handling and perhaps even more serious consequences in an accident – is a good reason to avoid these cabriolets. Apart from this, originality should be at the top of your priorities when buying a classic Lotus, and a Plus 2 cabriolet is clearly not as it left the factory. Colin Chapman never planned a drophead Plus 2, and the car was designed only as a fixed-head.

Relative values of the various Plus 2 versions are predictable, with the earliest cars being the cheapest and the big-valve model with five-speed gearbox the most expensive.

As a general rule, though, condition is now more important than age, and there is no substitute for looking at as many cars as you can before buying so as to gain a good 'feel' for pricing. The best cars sit very much in the same price bracket as the best Elans, and are a whisker more valuable than the equivalent Europas.

As long as you apply all the checks and advice outlined in the Elan chapter when looking for a Plus 2, you shouldn't come a cropper. Bear in mind, as always, that if a fully and competently restored Plus 2 is beyond your budget, consider very carefully whether restoration costs are going to turn that bargain into a rip-off.

Steer clear of cabriolet conversions. Apart from the fact that originality becomes increasingly crucial to any car's value as the years go by, there are major question marks about the safety implications of taking the lid off a Plus 2.

Like the Elan, all new body sections are available for the Plus 2 from the factory. On this car a new nose piece has been bonded to the body and filler applied to the join.

It may be little more than a longer and wider Elan, but the Plus 2 has completely different, and even more rakish, lines.

The Plus 2 is the most luxurious of the Lotuses in this book, with comprehensive instrumentation, burr walnut veneer dashboard and reasonable room for two adults.

Belinda Wilkins' Plus 2S 130 is a thoroughly useable daily car, chosen in preference to any other Lotus because she has two young children.

The Europa Special is a complete drivers' car. Motor's road test summed up its capabilities as, 'Good performance; fabulous handling and roadholding; excellent ride; relaxed at high speed'.

After a difficult birth in Renault-engined form, the Europa finally fulfilled its potential when the big-valved twin-cam engine was offered in 1972.

Peter Fouracres' Europa Special is just the kind of car that Lotus enthusiasts dream of owning. He bought it new and has kept it entirely original and perfectly maintained.

Europa

SPECIFICATIONS	Europa S1 and S2	Europa Twin Cam
Engine	In-line four	In-line four
Construction	Die-cast aluminium block and head	Cast-iron block, alloy head
Bore/stroke	76.0 x 81.0mm (Federal spec 77.0 x 84.0mm)	82.55 x 72.75mm
Capacity	1470cc (Federal spec 1565cc)	1558cc
Valves	Pushrod ohv	Double ohc
Compression ratio	10.25:1	9.5:1
Fuel system	Twin-choke downdraught Solex carburettor	Twin Weber 40DCOE or twin Dell'Orto DHLA40 carburettors
Power	82bhp at 6000rpm (Federal spec 80bhp at 6000rpm)	105bhp at 5500rpm
Torque	79lb ft at 4000rpm (Federal spec n/a)	103lb ft at 4500rpm
Transmission	Four-speed manual	Four-speed manual
Final drive	3.56:1	3.56:1
Brakes	Girling 9¼in front discs, 8 x 1¼in rear drums (servo optional)	Girling 9¼in front discs, 8 x 1¼in rear drums (servo standard)
Suspension front	Ind. by double wishbones, coil springs, telescopic dampers, anti-roll bar	Ind. by double wishbones, coil springs, telescopic dampers, anti-roll bar
Suspension rear	Ind. by trailing radius arms, lower link, fixed length drive-shafts, coil springs, telescopic dampers	Ind. by trailing radius arms, lower link, fixed length drive-shafts, coil springs, telescopic dampers
Steering	Rack and pinion	Rack and pinion
Wheels/tyres	Bolt-on 4½J steel wheels, 155 x 13 tyres	Bolt-on 4½J steel wheels, 155 x 13 tyres (optional bolt-on 5½J alloy wheels with 175-70 x 13 front and 185-70 x 13 rear tyres)
Body/chassis	Glass-fibre reinforced plastic body, steel box-section backbone chassis	Glass-fibre reinforced plastic body, steel box-section back bone chassis

DIMENSIONS

	Europa S1 and S2	Europa Twin Cam
Length	13ft 1in	13ft 1½in
Width	5ft 4½in	5ft 4½in
Height	3ft 6in	3ft 6in
Wheelbase	7ft 7in	7ft 8in
Unladen weight	1465lb	1588lb

SPECIFICATIONS

Europa Special

Engine	In-line four
Construction	Cast iron block, alloy head
Bore/stroke	82.55 x 72.75mm
Capacity	1558cc
Valve	Double ohc
Compression ratio	10.3:1
Fuel system	Twin Weber 40DCOE or twin Dell'Orto DHLA40 carburettors
Power	126bhp at 6500rpm
Torque	113lb ft at 5500rpm
Transmission	Five-speed manual
Final drive	3.77:1
Brakes	Girling 9¼in front discs, 8 x 1½in rear drums (servo standard)
Suspension front	Ind. by double wishbones, coil springs, telescopic dampers, anti-roll bar
Suspension rear	Ind. by trailing radius arms, lower link, fixed length, drive-shafts, coil springs, telescopic dampers
Steering	Rack and pinion
Wheels/tyres	Bolt-on 4½J alloy wheels, 155 x 13 tyres (optional bolt-on 5½J alloy wheels with 175-70 x 13 front and 185-70 13 rear tyres)
Body/chassis	Glass-fibre reinforced plastic body, steel box-section back-bone chassis

DIMENSIONS

Length	13ft 1½in
Width	5ft 4½in
Height	3ft 6in
Wheelbase	7ft 8in
Unladen weight	1588lb

Buried beneath its ancillaries is the 1470cc Renault engine and gearbox of an S2. The vee of the chassis and the cross-member over the gearbox can be seen clearly. The rarity of new Renault parts makes engine overhaul difficult nowadays.

Twin-cam models gained a little luggage space behind the engine. This Federal model has twin Zenith-Stromberg carburettors with crossover pipes to supply a little warm air to them.

The twin-cam engine is a tight fit in the Europa, with water pump end hard against the cockpit bulkhead. The large pulley on the end of the nearer camshaft is a modification over front-engined twin-cams needed to drive the alternator in its new position.

Announced in 1966, the mid-engined Europa took its name because it was designed as a 'Lotus for Europe' – indeed, it wasn't available in Britain until the S2 came on stream three years later. Although the Europa was praised for its technical innovation and unparalleled handling, Lotus enthusiasts never really accepted it until the wonderful twin-cam engine was installed in 1971. In the end, however, it did well in sales terms, a production run of 8469 making it the most popular Lotus after the Elan.

It really was a radical little machine, arriving at a time when only Lamborghini and Matra were producing mid-engined cars. While it was chalk against the Elan's cheese,

there were similarities in the design thinking and construction, Lotus staying faithful to glass-fibre bodywork, a steel backbone chassis and independent suspension all round. Performance wasn't as good as the Elan's at first, but by the time the Europa Special arrived in 1972 with 126bhp of big-valve twin-cam on board it had blossomed into a 121mph machine capable of 0-60mph in 6.6secs. In every way, as we shall see, the twin-cam cars make the best sense for today's classic car buyer who wants a Lotus with a difference.

Engine

For the first five years of production the Europa was offered with two types of Renault engines, which were then superseded by the ubiquitous twin-cam. When the car was launched, even more surprising than its mid-engined configuration was this installation of a French engine and gearbox, but it made sense for two reasons. First, the Europa was intended to sell chiefly in Europe where French parts would allow easier servicing, and, secondly, it was an advantage for Lotus – like any other small manufacturer – not to be totally dependent on one source, Ford, for major components.

The engine and gearbox unit of the front wheel drive Renault 16 was technically attractive because it needed so little modification to drive the rear wheels. It was simply turned about-face, with the gearbox behind the engine, and the crownwheel moved to the other side of the pinion so that the Europa could have four forward gears instead of four reverse ones! Conveniently, all belt drives and ancillaries were already positioned on the flywheel side of the engine, making them easily accessible in the centre of the Europa's engine bay instead of squeezed up against the cockpit bulkhead. The Renault Europa is rather easier to work on than the twin-cam Europa, which has its camshaft drive and water pump hard up by the bulkhead.

The Renault engine's combined block and crankcase is made from die-cast aluminium, and carries a five-bearing crankshaft. A single chain-driven camshaft sits at the top of the block, operating the valves through short pushrods and rockers. With the crankshaft nose buried in the transaxle casing, belt drive for the water pump and alternator instead comes off this high camshaft. A skew gear halfway along the camshaft drives a vertical shaft with the distributor beautifully accessible at its top and the oil pump lower down.

Cast-iron cylinder liners are held down by the aluminium head.

While its power output as installed in French tin boxes was a humble 59bhp, in mildly tuned form for the Europa this 1470cc (76 x 81mm bore and stroke) engine gave 78bhp at 6000rpm thanks to a higher 10.25:1 compression ratio, larger inlet valves and better porting. A Solex twin-choke down-draught carburettor was fitted. For the USA there was a slightly larger 1565cc (77 x 84mm bore and stroke) emissions version of this engine giving 80bhp at 6000rpm.

Although this Renault engine was reasonably pleasant and powerful, the Europa Twin-Cam with the basic 105bhp tune engine came along in 1971. Re-engineering to mate the twin-cam to Renault's four-speed gearbox was quite straightforward, consisting of the insertion of a Lotus-made bellhousing. This carried the alternator, now driven by a large pulley on the inlet camshaft. The Europa Special with the 126bhp big-valve unit follo-wed a year later when Renault were able to supply their stronger five-speed gearbox.

The Renault engine is an extremely reli-able, free-revving unit, but spare parts for the 1470cc version (dropped by Renault in 1970) are now a major problem. Apart from some of the ancillaries – water and oil pumps, distributor, etc – and gasket sets and valves, very little is available. As almost all the parts were common to the Renault 16, scrapyards may yield engines containing useful items, but most of these cars met their maker long ago. Consequently, many people have car-ried out a conversion to the 1565cc Renault 16TS unit, but from the purist's point of view a standard engine is preferable.

Where an ill-maintained engine has suffer-ed cooling problems, perhaps caused by the radiator silting up because of aluminium cor-rosion in the waterways, the head may have been skimmed so much that its life is limited. You can't check this on your inspection, but you can make sure that there is anti-freeze in the cooling system, that there's no oil in the water, and that the temperature is around 90°. Oil pressure should read around 40psi when running at 50mph, and there should be no blueness in the exhaust. The Solex car-burettor is a weak point as it leaks air through every pore after a few years in ser-vice, and an original fitment is now virtually useless. Lumpy tickover and sluggish per-formance are the symptoms to look for. A Renault engine fitted with alternative carbur-ettors, often Webers, is no bad thing as the Solex was cheap and inadequate.

In short, if you really do want to buy a Renault-engined Europa – and price is the only reason for choosing one instead of a twin-cam model – you must be absolutely sure about the engine's health. To be honest, there's no substitute for low mileage and a good service record, and as such cars are very rare perhaps you should think again about saving up for a twin-cam. All the checks for this engine are outlined in the Elan chapter.

Gearbox and rear axle

Three gearboxes of Renault origin – Types 336 and 352 were both four-speeds, the 365 a five-speed – were fitted to the Europa, deli-vered to the factory as complete units. As we've explained, the gearbox is mounted be-hind the engine and final drive to form a transaxle.

All Renault-engined models and the federal twin-cam used the Type 336 'box. This has a die-cast aluminium casing containing a gear cluster of the two-shaft kind and a hypoid crownwheel and pinion. Final drive ratio is 3.56:1, and the four synchromesh gears are on 3.61, 2.25, 1.48 and 1.03:1 ratios. Be-cause the gear selectors are right at the back of the 'box, a long and rather vague linkage is required. At first the linkage used plastic ball joints, but as these wore out quickly and ulti-mately separated, metal joints were intro-duced within a year of the Europa's launch. Europa Twin-Cams were fitted with the Type 352 'box, which was a little stronger but kept the same ratios. The extra big-valve power of the Europa Special required a stronger 'box, so in came the beefed-up Type 365 five-speed from the Renault 16TX, with ratios of 3.61, 2.33, 1.61, 1.21 and 0.87:1 and a 3.77:1 final drive. The only change Lotus made was to raise top gear to improve cruising ability.

All of these gearboxes are robust, but their linkages involve a tortuous series of shafts. The gearchange was never very pre-cise or quick at the best of times, but a parti-cularly awkward change will mean a linkage problem. Check that all the spherical joints and universal couplings in the linkage are tight and greased, and that all the rods look as if they are assembled in the right order. The linkage is set low enough to be seen clearly from underneath the car, so make sure that everything is straight – this low clearance can result in damage from kerbs or 'sleeping policemen'.

The gearbox and differential are unlikely to be noisy, but severe wear to gear teeth, syn-chromesh rings and crownwheel and pinion, generally caused by a sloppy linkage, is a serious black mark indicated by the usual symptoms of whining and synchromesh graunching. Apart from a few gaskets and seals, no parts whatsoever are available from Renault or Lotus, so a quiet 'box is essential. Specialist gear-cutting firms can solve the problem, but this is expensive. The driveshafts have to be shimmed up correctly where they go into the gearbox, so with the rear of the car jacked up check that there is no in-out play on the wheels. Don't be tempted by Europas which have had modern Renault Fuego 'boxes fitted, as this detracts from both originality and value.

The clutch is a Borg and Beck spring-diaphragm unit which will feel slightly heavy in operation because of its long cable. There is plenty of it to stretch, so free play should be checked every 3000 miles.

Suspension, steering and brakes

Although the Europa's front suspension is largely the same as that of the Elan, at the rear it is quite different. As on the Elite, fixed-length driveshafts form the upper links, while a single lower link on each side connects with the hub housing and bellhousing. A massive steel box-section trailing arm on each side – quite unlike any previous Lotus – anchors to the chassis in line with the cockpit bulkhead. A steel cross-beam bolted to the chassis and passing over the top of the gearbox provides the top mounting points for the spring-damper units.

At the front, there are cranked lower wishbones and upper wishbones pivoting on long fulcrum bolts, which also form the mountings for the top of the spring/damper units and the links to the low-set anti-roll bar. As on the Elan, a Triumph Herald upright

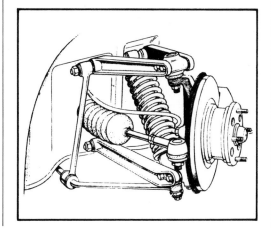

Front suspension sketch shows wishbone layout broadly similar to the Elan's. One long bolt takes care of top wishbone, spring/damper and anti-roll bar link mountings, while the upright is supported by a ball joint at the top and a trunnion below.

swivels in trunnions below and ball-joints at the top. The steering rack is a lengthened version of the Elan's Herald-derived Alford & Adler rack and pinion, but the coupling to the Herald column is different on the twin-cam cars, and common to the Elite/Eclat range.

Europa and Elan share the same 9½in Girling front discs, but at the rear there are 8 x 1¼in Girling drums (increased to 1½in width for the Europa Special). Unlike the Elan, brakes are mounted conventionally, next to the wheels, not on the inboard side of the uprights. Buyers of Renault-engined Europas could specify a servo, but this was standard on the twin-cam cars. Dull looking Elan bolt-on 4½J steel wheels with chrome hub caps and 155 x 13 tyres were the normal wear for Renault Europas, but the twin-cams brought the option of meatier 175/70 x 13 front and 185/70 x 13 rear tyres on 5½J alloy rims (standard fitting for the Special).

As there are no worries about obtaining suspension, steering or braking parts, any shortcomings here are not of great importance. Make the usual checks, nonetheless, starting with rocking the car at each corner to see that the springs and dampers are in good order. Rear dampers are more likely to be worn out because of the 56/44 rear-biased weight distribution. The large box-section trailing arms are prone to corrosion, particularly near the mounting points. All suspension components should be undamaged, but pay special attention to the front anti-roll bar as this is mounted very low. Indeed, the whole car is so low that an owner who has made a habit of parking on pavements may have bent lower suspension arms or weakened mounting points, and even if this is not visible irregular tyre wear will be an obvious clue. All rubber bushes should be tight and unperished – engine or gearbox oil leaks may have affected those at the rear.

Brakes are rarely a problem on Europas, so as long as the car stops well on your road test you should be all right. Remember that a Renault Europa probably won't have a servo. Steering should have no play or vibration, so if there is you should suspect worn track rod ends or a dry rack caused by the oil leaking away through split gaiters.

Body and chassis

The chassis principle introduced on the Elan, with the body straddling the steel box-section backbone, was carried over to the Europa, the mid-engined location allowing some simplification. The engine and gearbox

sit in a broad fork at the rear, while the front of the chassis is T-shaped, the ends of the simple cross-member incorporating suspension mounting points. Different patterns of tubes and mounting plates are used at the rear to accommodate the three Renault transmissions.

Although it doesn't have the Elan's pop-up headlamps, the bodyshell is superbly aerodynamic, with a drag coefficient of 0.32. On the S1 and S2 cars, large buttresses from the doors back to the tail give a 'bread van' appearance, but these were cut down – giving a slightly better rearward view – for the Twin-Cam and Special models. In order to retain the old weight distribution with the 40lb heavier twin-cam engine, the wheelbase (and overall length) was stretched by 1in. Mid-engined cars are notoriously impractical from the luggage space point of view, but the Europa was better than most with a total capacity of 4.8cu ft in the nose and tail compartments. An inadequate seven gallon fuel tank sat in the nearside forward corner of the engine compartment on the Renault Europas, balanced by the battery on the other side, but 12½ gallons' capacity in two tanks (with two filler caps and an interconnecting

pipe) arrived for some late Renault-engined models and all the twin-cam cars.

All the ground-rules outlined in the Elan chapter apply equally to the Europas, although the chassis is generally more durable on these models. There is one exception, however, for the straight crossmember at the front is more vulnerable to corrosion. Road dirt penetrates the chassis holes in the area of the steering rack mountings and master cylinders, causing internal rot. Unfortunately, this corrosion is difficult to identify,

Europa chassis follows Lotus principles, but forms a T at the front. Frames are not interchangeable because different mounting plates are needed for the three engine/gearbox permutations.

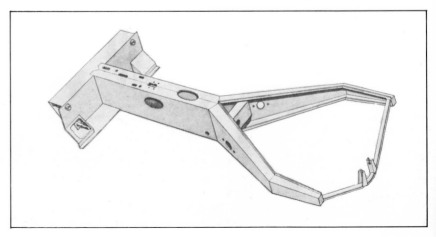

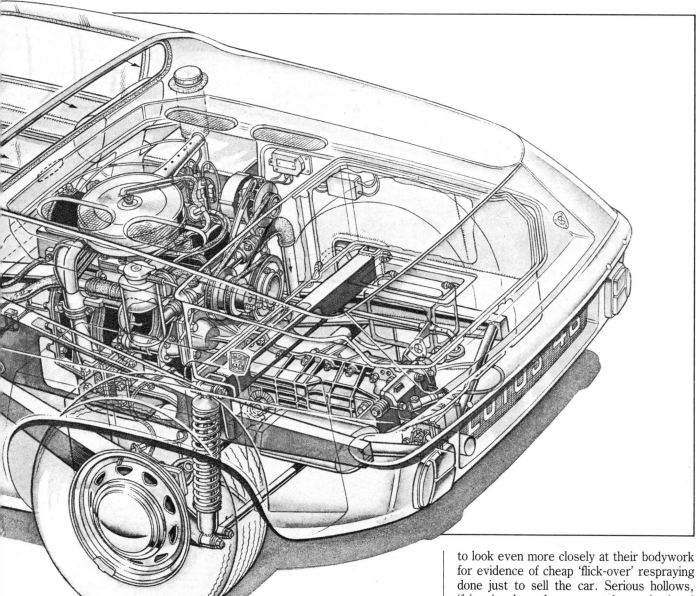

above
Autocar cutaway shows the original – and now highly problematical – Europa S1. It is the least desirable of all the Lotuses covered in this book, and the way in which its bodyshell is bonded, rather than bolted, to the chassis makes it a restoration headache today. Thankfully, there are very few in Britain! Note the longitudinal mounting of the Renault engine and gearbox, the familiar backbone chassis structure and the massive box section swing axle rear suspension.

although the consequences are serious – the brake master cylinder and the steering rack can break away from the chassis. Another problem with this crossmember is that the strip of felt along its top surface cushioning the bodywork absorbs water, causing rust. At the rear, look carefully for any signs of accident distortion of the Y-shaped forks, as this will affect the suspension geometry. If the alignment is not true, a new chassis will be necessary as rectification of any damage is unwise. Even a chassis problem as minor as distorted fulcrum pins will require replacement.

Since Renault-engined Europas are much less valuable that Elans or Plus 2s, you need to look even more closely at their bodywork for evidence of cheap 'flick-over' respraying done just to sell the car. Serious hollows, 'fairy rings', sandpaper scratches and painted over gel-cracks will mean that thorough surface preparation, possibly stripping back to bare glass-fibre, will be needed prior to a proper respray. In really bad instances, this could cost as much as the purchase price of the car. As long as you are aware of the cost, damaged body sections present no problem as everything for all Europa models is still available from the factory.

Europa Special sills have a fine aluminium flake in the gel coat. This is not a painted finish, and very difficult to recreate if it has discoloured. Renault Europas had a rubber windscreen surround with a chrome infill strip, and if damaged this can still be obtained, but late S2 models onwards had a bonded screen which is more expensive to replace. No car left the factory with a sun-roof fitted, and the roof and windscreen pillar cracking that this can cause is a good reason for rejecting a car so fitted. Forget the old stories about debris being sucked through an open sunroof – structural strength is far more important.

If you're thinking of buying an S1 Europa, there's one simple piece of advice: don't! As the chassis is bonded to the body the problems are mind-boggling when it's rotten, which all will be by now. The body has to be physically cut away from the old chassis and fitted to a new S2 chassis – it's a phenomenal task.

Interior

Once again, the S1s are the least desirable Europas when it comes to interior trim and equipment. Their worst fault is fixed side windows – truly claustrophobic in summer! The thinking behind them was rational enough, for Colin Chapman planned an elaborate system whereby the front luggage compartment would have an air-tight rubber seal around its opening, allowing it to be pressurised in order to provide exemplary ventilation. Air was fed through three outlets into the cockpit, one being a heater matrix, the other two Renault butterfly nozzles at either end of the facia. Seats were fixed on the floor but a telescopic steering column provided a degree of flexibility, while the back rests reclined.

S2 interiors were much better, thanks in part to electrically operated door windows and better seats with fore/aft movement. The dashboard had a straight grain polished veneer finish, and into it were set a full complement of instruments: speedometer and tachometer were ahead of the driver, while a row of four smaller dials in the centre registered fuel, temperature, oil pressure and battery charge. All Renault Europas had black vinyl upholstery and full carpeting. The only stowage space was a small glovebox and two door pockets. The S1's single windscreen wiper was retained.

The civilizing process went a stage further with the Twin-Cam. Lotus engineers managed to find a little more room in the footwells, the cockpit floor was lowered slightly and better sound deadening material covered the rear bulkhead. An attractive oatmeal trim colour became an option on the twin-cam cars, with the last of the line Europa Specials having cord inserts in the seats.

Check the interior carefully for rips and burns. Blemishes are no real problem on black trim as it is relatively easy and cheap to

repair, but on oatmeal cars the precise material is difficult to obtain. Don't worry about a grubby oatmeal interior as a good valeting should bring this back to life, but if all the trim looks new make sure that it is in the authentic material – the chances are that it won't be, and the genuine oatmeal is expensive. Any dashboard wrinkling or damage can't really be repaired as the veneer is so thin, but a new dashboard (time-consuming to fit) can be substituted or new veneer applied. New headlining can be obtained, and is simple to fit as it is stuck to the roof, not held by wires as on the Plus 2s and fixed-head Elans.

Make sure that the windscreen rubber surround is in good order as leaks are common, with detrimental effect on interior trim. Don't worry if the electric windows seem sluggish – they were always like that! The mechanism and motors (windscreen wiper units from the Ford Anglia!) are generally reliable.

Restoration

Apart from the fact that Renault engine and gearbox parts are like gold dust, Europas present no more restoration headaches than Elans. What you must bear in mind, however, is that Renault-powered cars are pretty undesirable by Lotus standards, so wholesale professional restoration just isn't cost-effective. If you're really capable, on the other hand, restoring a ratty Renault Europa could be the cheapest way to own a classic Lotus.

Refurbishment of the twin-cam models is very much easier as these cars are still relatively young. Tired gearboxes are a problem, but the twin-cam is a rugged unit which should go on forever if properly rebuilt. It's covered fully in the Elan chapter.

While twin-cam Europa chassis are available as official Lotus replacement parts, those for the Renault-powered Europas are made under licence (by Fibreglass Services in Sussex). Just as with the Elan, chassis replacement is inevitable sooner or later, but relatively few twin-cam Europas have yet reached this point. The only way to deal with a rotten chassis on an S1 is to cut the bodywork away and fit an S2 replacement. This is a very time-consuming task – suddenly the glorious advantages of a glass-fibre car seem to vanish!

When renovating a Europa bodyshell, once again balance the cost or effort of stripping and repainting engine or nose lids against buying new ones – the latter could be cheaper if you have a professional do the work. Damaged bumpers cause no headaches as the front one comes from the Ford Anglia, the rear from the Cortina. All suspension, steering and brake parts are still available.

As the Europa's total production run exceeded 9000, only the Elan is more prolific. This, together with the relative youth of the twin-cam models, means that Europas in reasonable mechanical health are no more difficult to restore.

Maintenance

The maintenance schedules are basically the same for Renault and twin-cam Europas. Change engine oil and the oil filter every 3000 miles, check the tappets and change plugs and points every 6000, and replace air filters at 12,000. As with the twin-cam, internal corrosion is minimized on the Renault engines by using anti-freeze all the year round.

Do treat the gearbox gently because of the absence of spare parts, and make sure the linkage is always tight and greased. The transaxle's oil level should be checked every 3000 miles, and replenished with EP80 oil every 6000. One point to remember is that the Europa's fixed-length driveshafts physically come out of the gearbox, and behind the roll-pins which retain the driveshafts to the 'box are shims. Exaggerated wear will take place if this assembly isn't shimmed up correctly, and by now you should have the message about replacing gearbox parts...

On the suspension side, front links and driveshafts should be greased every 3000 miles, while the steering rack nipple needs to be greased every 12,000. With the engine up at the back, make sure that oil leaks don't perish the rubber suspension bushes. Rear-biased weight distribution means that the back dampers will have a shorter life than the front ones. Although the front disc brakes have the same calipers as Elans, they carry a different type of pad material. The adjuster nut on the rear drums, with different brake shoes for the Special, must be kept lubricated. Re-kitting or replacing the brake master cylinder is an awkward job as it is buried in the nose through the chassis, and also has a remote tank.

Cost guidelines

As they are the Cinderellas of the range, Europa S1s and S2s are quite cheap, running examples being available at prices which

Practicality is not the Europa's strongest suit. In fact, a suit is about all that will fit in the front compartment.

The Europa S2's interior was neatly, but not sumptuously, trimmed. The glovebox has no lid, but instrumentation is comprehensive and the dashboard is finished with a grained wood veneer. Twin-cam models were a little more luxurious, but the layout was much the same.

As with the Plus 2, oatmeal trim is the most desirable specification. Some agility is required to enter the car, but the seats provide good support.

would buy only a broken Elan. Their restoration is no cheaper, however, and the bonded chassis/body of the S1 presents special problems – thankfully, almost all S1s were exported! Because even the best Renault Europas are worth no more than a very humble, tired Elan, the only way restoration can pay is by doing all the work yourself.

Twin-cam Europas are a different kettle of fish. Their prices are buoyant, falling not far short of equivalent condition Elans. A Europa Special in John Player Special colours is the most desirable of the lot because it is the youngest model, and the big-valve engine gives supercar performance even by today's standards. Unless you pay a vastly inflated price for a twin-cam, you should never lose money.

S2 Europas kept the S1's ungainly high rear buttresses and Renault mechanicals, but became more civilized thanks to electrically-operated side windows. The quarter-lights are a recognition feature – S1s have fixed single-pane windows.

Far more collectable are the twin-cam Europas, this 105bhp model being called, simply, the Twin Cam. It is instantly distinguishable from Renault-powered cars by its cut-down tail area and small chin spoiler – the alloy wheels were an option which most buyers specified.

The best Europa of all is the Special, visually identifiable by badging, a pinstripe paint scheme and a neater sill line. This car is finished in the John Player Special black and gold colours of Lotus's Formula 1 sponsor. The twin fuel fillers are a feature of all twin-cam Europas.

Left-hand drive and side indicator repeaters identify this as a Federal Europa Special. The gear linkage can be seen at the rear of the car.

In a nutshell

Unlike any other Lotus, there's a Europa for all pockets. You couldn't buy a running Elan, Plus 2 or even a Seven for the price of a tolerably good Renault Europa, but the best Europa Specials come near the top of the Lotus price scale. There's a reason for this, of course, and by now you should have the message: the Renault-powered cars just don't have the charisma of the twin-cams, and engine and gearbox breakages are bad news on the parts front.

That said, Europas have a unique appeal. They may not be the centre of attention at club gatherings, but they turn more heads in the High Street than any Elan or Plus 2. Their handling is even better than the Elan's, they are more luxurious, the five-speed Special is a much better high-speed cruiser and the Grand Prix car mechanical layout is technically more interesting.

Think very carefully before buying a Renault Europa, and let mechanical health dictate your decision. Seek a specialist's opinion of a car before you part with any money, as restoration costs could far outweigh the gain in value. If you can afford to, don't consider a Renault Europa – you can't go far wrong with a Twin-Cam or Special.

Oddly enough, the Europa was never used seriously in motor racing even though its mid-engined configuration was inspired by Formula 1 practice. This is Andrew Wroughton's 'Prodsports' racer at Brands Hatch in 1981.

Production History

Seven

OCTOBER 1957

First Seven launched with 1172cc Ford sidevalve engine and all-aluminium bodywork with cyclewings at front. 40bhp standard, but 48bhp tune and close-ratio gears optional. Price £1036 inclusive of taxes, but most sold in kit form at £536. Chassis nos begin at £400.

DECEMBER 1958

Coventry Climax FWA 75bhp 1098cc Super Seven announced, with wire wheels, wooden steering wheel and tachometer as standard (but speedometer optional). Kit price £892, fully assembled £1546.

OCTOBER 1959

Seven A with 37bhp 948cc BMC A-series engine and BMC gearbox introduced. US sales begin with same engine in 'Frogeye' Sprite 43bhp tune, and indicators and better trim. Kit price now £511. Production transfers from Hornsey to Cheshunt.

JUNE 1960

S2 models introduced with same Ford and BMC engines, but Standard rear axle and lighter chassis. American Seven A could be specified with optional 1098cc Sprite engine. Fuel tank now steel instead of aluminium, hood, wipers and spare wheel all now standard, flared front wings and nosecone in glass fibre. Kit prices £611 (Seven A) and £587 (Seven F). Chassis nos begin SB1000.

JANUARY 1961

BMC and Ford sidevalve engines superseded by 39bhp 997cc ohv Ford Anglia 105E engine and gearbox. New A-frame rear suspension. Kit price drops to £499.

JULY 1961

New Super Seven appears with Cosworth-modified 109E Classic 1340cc ohv engine and 109E gearbox. Power 85bhp. Sidescreens become an option. Kit price £599.

SEPTEMBER 1962

Super Seven 1500 launched with 116E Cortina 1498cc ohv engine and Cortina GT all-synchro gearbox. 66bhp standard, 95bhp for optional Cosworth tune. Front discs appear. Kit price £585, Cosworth £645. Options include heater, tonneau, indicators and oil cooler. New full-length exhaust, hood with rear quarter-light windows and sealed beam dipping headlights.

OCTOBER 1966

All Lotus production, including Sevens, moves to Hethel, starting at chassis no SB2102.

AUGUST 1968

S3 introduced with 225E ohv crossflow engine in 84bhp 1598cc (Cortina) and 72bhp 1297cc (Escort) versions. 116E gearbox retained, rear axle now from Escort. New facia with tachometer standard, some of previous optional equipment (indicators, sidescreens, electric fan) standard. 1600 usually specified, at £775 in kit form. Chassis nos start SC2311.

JANUARY 1969	One-off Seven S built for Racing Car Show with 120bhp Holbay-modified 1598cc Ford engine. Full spec included leather steering wheel, full carpets, air horns etc.
OCTOBER 1969	Lotus 1558cc twin-cam engine first fitted. Only 13 built, all with Holbay-tuned 125bhp engine, stronger chassis and better trim. Rear lights recessed in wings. Brand Lotus alloy wheels standard. Kit price £1250.
MARCH 1970	Glass-fibre S4 launched with same Ford engines plus twin-cam (with 125bhp Holbay option) and Corsair 2000E gearbox. New Watts linkage rear suspension, tubular chassis with steel panels. Better hood, sidescreens with sliding perspex panels. Options include heater, roll bar, alloy wheels and screen washers. Kit prices £895 (1600) and £1245 (twin-cam) Chassis nos start 2650.
MAY 1973	Caterham Car Sales take over S4 production. Chassis nos begin 3501.
APRIL 1974	First Caterham S3 built with stronger chassis and 126bhp big-valve twin-cam, chassis no CS3/3551/TCR.
SEPTEMBER 1974	Caterham S3 officially introduced, price £1540 in kit form only (although purchase tax now abolished).

ELITE

OCTOBER 1957	First Elite displayed at Earls Court Motor Show, but still not ready for production. This car later broken up.
MAY 1958	The first of 10 prototypes built at Edmonton delivered to Ian Walker, one of several customers to race cars this season. Chassis numbers start at EA/1001.
OCTOBER 1958	Full-scale Elite production begins in new factory at Cheshunt, using bodyshells supplied by Maximar. Coventry Climax 1216cc FWE engine fitted with single SU carburettor, producing 78bhp. A few cars had twin SUs. MG gearbox. Price including taxes £1951.
JULY 1960	Series 2 model introduced with transfer of body production to Bristol Aircraft Company. Design changes include rear suspension wishbone in place of trailing link, softer spring rates, Pirelli or Michelin tyres in place of Firestones. EB/1251 introduces new chassis no sequence. Price £2006, but now available in kit form at £1299.
OCTOBER 1960	Special Equipment version arrives, with 83bhp engine on twin SUs and close-ratio ZF gearbox as standard.
MAY 1962	Lotus introduce Super 95, 100 and 105 conversions, figures denoting power outputs.
MAY 1964	Last Elite produced.

ELAN

OCTOBER 1962

Elan 1500 presented at Earls Court Motor Show, priced at £1499 or £1095 in kit form. Official Lotus designation is Type 26. New glass-fibre convertible body style with pop-up headlamps, separate steel backbone chassis. Ford based twin-cam engine, all independent suspension, Ford four-speed gearbox. Chassis nos begin 26/0001.

MAY 1963

1558cc (105bhp) twin-cam replaces 1500cc unit – all 22 cars with smaller engine recalled to have 1558cc engine installed. Optional hard-top offered.

NOVEMBER 1964

S2 introduced from chassis on 26/3900. New integral tail lamp treatment, larger front brake calipers, new veneer facia with lockable glovebox, smaller pedal pads, quick-release fuel filler. Knock-on steel wheels optional.

SEPTEMBER 1965

S3 fixed-head coupe introduced, now with Type 36 designation, from chassis no 36/4510. Battery moved from cockpit to boot, boot lid extended to tail panel, electric operation for windows. Convertible continued in S2 form, with 26 prefix for chassis nos.

JANUARY 1966

Special Equipment package offered on S2 convertible from chassis no 26/5282. 115bhp engine, 3.55:1 final drive. Closeratio gearbox, servo brakes and knock-on wheels standard. Repeater flashers on front wings.

JUNE 1966

S2/S3 rationalization completed. S3 convertible with Type 45 designation joins existing S3 fhc, having same modifications plus improved hood and framed door windows. Last S2 convertible is 26/5810, last S2 Special Equipment convertible is 26/5798. S3 convertibles start at 45/5701.

JULY 1966

Special Equipment also available on S3 fhc (from 36/5977). Prices now as follows: fhc, £1553 (£1262 in kit form); fhc S/E, £1711 (£1391); convertible, £1553 (£1262); convertible S/E, £1711 (£1391).

MARCH 1968

S4 convertible (from chassis no 45/7895) and fhc (from 36/7896) introduced. Distinguished by flared, squarer wheelarches to accept low profile tyres, larger rear lamps to Plus 2 style, bonnet bulge and Zenith-Stromberg carbs on all cars, perforated vinyl seat trim, rocker action for facia switches. Prices now as follows: fhc, £1732 (£1353 in kit form); fhc S/E, £1902 (£1486); convertible, £1732 (£1353); convertible S/E, £1902 (£1486).

DECEMBER 1969

Chassis nos on old system conclude at 36/9824 (fhc) and 45/9823 (convertible).

JANUARY 1970

New chassis nos start at 7001 010001 (first two figures indicate year, next two month). Suffix letters indicate body styles as follows; A, S4 fhc; C, S4 convertible; E, S4 S/E fhc; G, S4 S/E convertible.

OCTOBER 1970	S4 Sprint introduced with big-valve 126bhp engine. Two-tone colour scheme available with 'Elan Sprint' wording on dividing strip. Compression ratio raised to 10.3:1. Dell'Orto carbs at first, later Webers. Stronger final drive, driveshafts and Rotoflex couplings. Prices: £2162 (£1659 in kit form).
AUGUST 1973	Elan production discontinued.

PLUS 2

JUNE 1967	First designated Elan +2, this was a stretched version (12in more wheelbase, 7in more track, 3cwt heavier) with 2+2 seating. Twin-cam engine in 115bhp guise with Weber carbs. Four-speed Ford gearbox, 3.77:1 final drive, servo standard. Price £1923 (£1672 in kit form). Designated Type 50, chassis nos from 50/0001.
JANUARY 1969	US sales begin, with Zenith-Stromberg carbs throughout production run.
MARCH 1969	Plus 2S arrives from chassis no 50/1593, now not available in kit form. More luxurious interior, 118bhp and Zenith-Stromberg carbs, foglights. Price £2200.
DECEMBER 1969	'Base model' Plus 2 discontinued, 50/2407 last chassis no. Old chassis no system finishes with 50/2536 last Plus 2S.
JANUARY 1970	New chassis no system begins with L suffix.
OCTOBER 1970	Plus 2S replaced by Plus 2S 130 with 126bhp big-valve engine. Most cars have self-coloured silver roof. Price £2616
OCTOBER 1972	Plus 2S 130/5 arrives with five-speed gearbox.
DECEMBER 1974	Plus 2S 130 and 130/5 discontinued.

EUROPA

DECEMBER 1966	Launched for French market only with 1470cc Renault engine producing 78bhp at 6000rpm. Mid-engined two-seater fixed-head, with glass-fibre body bonded to steel backbone chassis for extra strength. Renault four-speed gearbox behind engine, 3.56:1 final drive. Fixed side windows. Designated Type 46, chassis nos start 46/0001.
FEBRUARY 1967	Deliveries of first 500 for France begin.
OCTOBER 1967	S1 Mk2 from chassis nos 46/0300 to 0644, with improved gearbox.

APRIL 1968	S2, or Type 54, launched in Europe. Chassis nos from 54/0645. Redesigned with detachable body, electric door windows, improved interior with veneered facia.
MARCH 1969	S2 launched in USA with 1565cc Renault engine producing 80bhp at 6000rpm from chassis no 54/1066. Ride height raised to meet bumper height regulations.
JUNE 1969	S2 becomes available in UK, price £1667 (£1275 in kit form).
NOVEMBER 1969	More serious entry into USA market with Type 65 version with higher wing line to meet regulations. Hard to spot the difference!
SEPTEMBER 1971	S2 phased out. Last chassis nos are 7105/120416P (UK), 7108/170425Q (export), 7112/411290R (USA). Final price £1918 (£1459 in kit form).
DECEMBER 1971	Twin-Cam, designated Type 74, launched in UK with 105bhp version of 1558cc twin-cam four-cylinder, 3.56:1 final drive. Wheelbase increased by 1in to improve cockpit room for tall drivers, tail buttresses cut down. More fuel capacity with 12½ galls in two tanks. Optional (for £101) alloy rims with larger tyres (175/70 front, 185/70 rear) usually fitted. Price £1995 (£1595 in kit form). Chassis nos begin 7109/181000P (UK), 7111/252001R (USA), 7201/011000Q (export).
SEPTEMBER 1972	Europa Special launched with 126bhp big-valve engine, five-speed gearbox, 3.77:1 final drive. Chassis nos begin 7208/1783P (UK), 7208/1101Q (export), 7208/2684R (USA). Price £2471 (£2044 in kit form).
APRIL 1975	Last Europa, chassis no 7504/2434P, produced.

Insurance

There is no point in even approaching the major insurance firms, with the exception of Norwich Union and Sun Alliance, as they are not interested in the classic market and will charge you the earth. Even the high street brokers are not always fully informed about all the policies available. But all is not lost.

You can obtain very reasonably priced comprehensive insurance either through Club Lotus or by approaching the two specialist classic car insurance brokers recommended by Club Lotus at the time of writing. These are Footman James and Company Limited, Waterfall Industrial Estate, Waterfall Lane, Cradley Heath, Warley, West Midlands B64 6PU (tel: 021 561 2847/8) and Clarkson Puckle West Midlands Limited, PO Box 27, Falcon House, The Minories, Dudley DY2 8PF (tel: 0384 455011).

Sensibly, they work out their premiums on the basis that you are going to treasure your car, and are fairly unlikely to damage it!

There is a variety of schemes for all kinds of owners, ranging from off-the-road cover for restoration projects to limited mileage premiums (usually 1500, 3000 or 6000 miles) and even unlimited mileage scales for those who use their cars regularly. Being over 25 is a distinct advantage, but more expensive cover is possible for the 21-24 age bracket. It is essential to take out an agreed value policy, so that in the unfortunate event of your car being written off you know that you will receive full compensation. The 'estimated value' you put on a conventional policy form is not the sum you receive in the event of a write-off – hundreds of classic car owners over the years have fallen into this trap. Club Lotus is invaluable in establishing an agreed value, for its secretary, Graham Arnold, and 'area leaders' are authorized by Footman James and Clarkson Puckle to assess the value of your car without necessarily having to inspect it.

Production Figures

Factory records are patchy, so most figures have to be quoted approximately. It is unlikely that more accuracy will ever be possible and it is impossible to break down the totals for each series.

	Number Built
Seven	
Lotus	3300 approx
Caterham	1200 approx
Elite	1048
Elan	12,224 approx
Plus 2	5200 approx
Europa	9230 approx

Clubs

The leading organization for owners of the 'first-generation' Lotuses covered in this book is **Club Lotus,** with around 4000 members. Run by Graham Arnold, a former sales director at Lotus, it has 23 area groups all over the country with more than 40 meetings of one kind and another taking place every month. Arnold is an expert on all aspects of the marque and produces an excellent quarterly magazine, *Club Lotus News.* The club, formed in 1956, is particularly strong on practical advice, issuing technical bulletins (for example, a three-page document about the twin-cam water pump) and organizing technical seminars given by Lotus-trained people – these services are free to members. Insurance – including valuation – can be arranged through the club (see above). Club Lotus is completely independent from the factory, and its top event is a national gathering at Castle Combe racing circuit every May. Details can obtained from PO Box 8, Dereham, Norfolk IP25 6AE (tel: 0362 4459).

There is also an official organisation, **Club Team Lotus,** run by Andrew Ferguson from the factory. Formed at Colin Chapman's instigation in 1982, it is angled more towards the modern cars and keeping members in touch with Lotus's factory activities and Formula 1 exploits, but it also publishes a slick colour magazine, *Lotus World,* every month. Membership is around 5000, and one of the most popular activities is an annual open day at Ketteringham Hall. Only official Lotus dealers and the eight Lotus classic dealers are recognised by this club. Find out more from Andrew Ferguson, Club Team Lotus, Lotus Marketing Services, Ketteringham Hall, Wymondham, Norfolk NR18 9RS (tel: 0603 811662).

Much smaller than either of these, but catering for all models, is the **Lotus Drivers Club,** founded in 1977. With a membership of around 700 centred in the Midlands, the club is particularly attractive to the competition minded Lotus owner. Several sprints are organized every year, as well as the usual concours d'elegance and pub meetings. The club has a list of recommended specialists and offers 'phone-in technical advice. A monthly magazine, *Chicane,* is sent to all members. For details, contact Jenny Barton Lee, 15 Pleasant Way, Leamington Spa, Warwickshire CU32 5XA.

Seven owners have their own organization, the **Lotus Seven Club,** which has 250 members. It started life back in 1967, was run for a while from Caterham Car Sales and is now flourishing under the guidance of David Mirylees. Its 250 members receive a monthly newsletter, and the highlight of their year is the annual international gathering, held in recent years at Oulton Park and Brands Hatch. Discount arrangements with major parts suppliers and preferential insurance rates are two of the club's practical benefits. Write for details to David Mirylees, 18 St James, Beaminster, Dorset. There is also a host of Ford and BMC clubs which could prove valuable in locating spares for owners of earlier Sevens. With these smaller clubs, officials tend to change frequently, so your best advice is to write for up to date information to *Classic and Sportscar* Editorial, Haymarket Publishing Ltd, 38-42 Hampton Road, Teddington, Middlesex TW11 0JE (tel: 01-977 8787).

Elite owners have their own group, **Club Elite,** run by the leading specialist for these cars (and all other Lotuses), Miles Wilkins. Founded in 1969, it has 170 members, around 100 of them British. Catering for such a rare car, it is invaluable to any Elite owner as a source of advice, knowledge and parts. Six professionally printed newsletters are produced every year, and a test day is held at Goodwood racing circuit every October. Particularly useful is the club's annually updated register of all known Elites. Details from Miles Wilkins, The Coach House, The Street, Walberton, Arundel, West Sussex (tel: 0243 551143).

Anyone with a pre-1961 Lotus might also like to contact the **Historic Lotus Register.** Victor Thomas runs this from Badgerswood, School Road, Drayton, Norwich NR8 6EF (tel: 0603 867464).

Specialists

There are plenty of Lotus specialists up and down the country, but some are better than others. The following names and addresses are a comprehensive listing, but it would be wise to seek recommendations from other Lotus owners before having any work done.

Restoration

Fibreglass Services, Charlton Sawmills, Charlton Singleton, Chichester, Sussex (tel: 0243 63320).

Daytune, Coldhams Road, Cambridge CB1 3EW (tel: 0223 211889).

Paul Matty Sports Cars, 12 Old Birmingham Road, Lickley Road, Bromsgrove, Worcs (tel: 0527 35656).

Christopher Neil Sportscars, Middlewich Road, Northwich, Cheshire CW9 7BP (tel: 0606 47914).

C.J. Foulds (Motors) Ltd. Commercial Mills, Frith Street, Huddersfield, W. Yorks (tel: 0484 534743).

Barry Ely Motors, 453 High Road, Leyton, London E10 (tel: 01 558 3221).

Robin Alabaster, Halfway Garage, Bath Road, Padworth, Berks (tel: 0734 712376).

Arnolds Garage, Shottermill Ponds, Haslemere, Surrey (tel: 0428 3192).

Automobile Workshop, Lancaster Mews, Richmond, Surrey (tel: 01 940 0593).

Vegantune Ltd, Cradge Bank, Spalding, Lincs PE11 3AB (tel: 0775 4846).

Norfolk Motor Co Ltd, Sprowston Road, Norwich, Norfolk (tel: 0603 416613).

Len Street Ltd, 67 Drayton Gardens, London SW10 (tel: 01 370 0611).

Kelvedon Motors, Bourne Road, Spalding, Lincs (tel: 0775 5457).

Soutar & Rhodes Ltd, Union Mills, Harrogate Road, Bradford BD2 35P (tel: 0274 630865/632736).

Terry Carthy, 4E Pepper Road, Bramhall Moor Ind Est, Hazel Grove, Stockport, Cheshire (tel: 061 456 5341).

Dave Gallop Auto Care, Unit 1, Heath Farm, Ironmould Lane, Brislington, Bristol BS4 5RD (tel: 0272 714968).

N.J.T. Developments, 10A Christchurch Street, West Frome, Somerset (tel: 0373 65822).

Westfield Cars, 5 Gibbons Park, Dudley Road, Kingswinford, W. Midlands (tel: 0384 279650).

Classic Transport Co, Rainbow Industrial Park, Old Fafnir Works, Littleworth Road, Hednesford, Staffs (tel: 05438 78501).

Eagle Racing, nr Maidstone, Kent (tel: 0622 843312).

Mick Miller, Carlton Cross, Kelsale, Saxmundham, Suffolk (tel: 0728 3307).

Parts and servicing

Bell & Colvill Ltd, Epsom Road, West Horsley, Surrey (tel: 04865 4671).

Mike Spence Ltd, School Green, Shinfield, Reading, Berks (tel: 0734 884545).

Caterham Car Sales, Seven House, Town End, Caterham Hill, Surrey (tel: 0883 42382).

Malmesbury Specialist Cars, Crudwell Road, Malmesbury, Wilts (tel: 06662 2309).

Morland Jones Ltd, 226-227 Trussley Road, Hammersmith, London W4 (tel: 01 741 2303).

The London Lotus Centre, Ballards Yard, High Street, Edgware, Middlesex (tel: 01 952 5578).

Northern Sportscars, Scorton, Richmond, N. Yorks DL10 6ED (tel: 0748 811613).

Yardley Wood Service Station, Yardley Wood Road, Birmingham (tel: 021 474 6981).

Lyte & Wakefield, 166 Bush Hill Park, Enfield, Middlesex (tel: 01 367 4192).

Mill Garage, Thorney, Peterborough, Cambs (tel: 0733 27044).

Spydersport Ltd, Station Road Ind Est, Whittlesey, Peterborough, Cambs (tel: 0733 203986).

Coupes of London, 25 Sheldon Road, London NW2 (tel: 01 452 6922).

Boss Motors, Snetterton, Norwich, Norfolk (tel: 095 387 471).

Arch Motors & Manufacturing Co, Red Wings Way, Huntingdon PE18 7HD (tel: 0480 59661).

Engines and transmissions

Burton Performance Centre Ltd, 623-631 Eastern Avenue, Barkingside, Ilford, Essex IG2 6PN (tel: 01 554 2281).

Quorn Engine Developments, Soar Road, Quorn, Leics (tel: 0509 412317).

Twincam Techniques, 7 Hinckley Park, Hinckley, Leics (tel: 0455 619006).

Nicol Transmissions, Coppice Trading Estate, Stourport Road, Kidderminster, Worcs DY11 7QY (tel: 0562 752651).

Dave Smith Racing Engines, 214A Wanstead Park Road, Ilford, Essex (tel: 01 554 4144).

E.M. Winter, 9 Witham Close, Bedford MK41 7YT (tel: 0234 68803).

Norvic Engines, Little Staughton Airfield, Bedford.

Vulcan Engineering Ltd, 185 Uxbridge Road, London W7 (tel: 01 579 3202).

Lynx Engines, 69 Dunston Park, Paignton, Devon (tel: 0803 527134).

Climax Engine Services, 82 Northwick Park Estate, Blockley, Glos GL56 9RF (tel: 0386 700631).

Author's Acknowledgements

I thought I knew a little bit about Lotuses before I started to write this book, but once I began talking to some of the leading restoration specialists I very quickly realized how much I had to learn. So it is that I owe a great debt to several people without whom this book would have many more shortcomings.

In particular I should like to thank Miles Wilkins of Fibreglass Services, the well-known specialist who lives, breathes and talks Lotus, and did so with me for two days. Further information about Elans came from Pat Thomas of Kelvedon Motors and Peter Day of Daytune. David Wakefield of Caterham Car Sales was invaluable in providing notes about Sevens, and David Mirylees of the Lotus Seven Club was also helpful. Tony Bates supplied a great deal of information for the Elite chapter. I am also grateful to the owners who brought out their cars on a cold winter day for colour photography: Miles Wilkins owns one of the best Elites in Britain and restored it seven years ago; his wife, Belinda, runs the Plus 2S130 as her day-to-day car; David Clark owns the Gold Leaf coloured Elan Sprint; Vincent Haydon's Seven Twin Cam SS, one of seven Lotuses in his collection, must be one of the best Sevens in the country; and Peter Fouracres' magnificent Europa Special looks as good as the day he bought it new 12 years ago. One of my *Classic and Sportscar* colleagues, Mick Walsh, worked solidly from dawn till dusk to produce such marvellous photographs. I am also indebted to Paul Dudley for stepping in at short notice to take most of the 'What to look for' photographs.

Any author relies to a small extent on the published work of historians before him, and Jeremy Coulter in particular was unknowingly of immense help through his splendid *The Lotus & Caterham Sevens,* without doubt the definitive story of these cars.

Picture Acknowledgements

The publishers are grateful to the following for supplying pictures reproduced in this book: Quadrant Picture Library; *Autocar, Autosport, Classic and Sportscar* (Haymarket Publishing Motoring Photo Library).

VIVA MILLE MIGLIA!
LAMBORGHINIS OLD & NEW ● LOTUS PROFILE
SPORTING ESTATES COMPARED

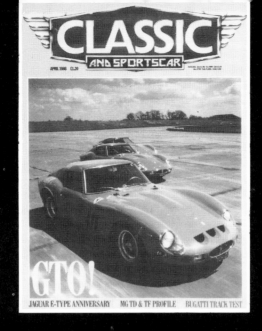

GTO!
JAGUAR E-TYPE ANNIVERSARY ● MG TD & TF PROFILE ● BUGATTI TRACK TEST

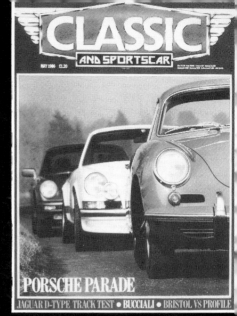

PORSCHE PARADE
JAGUAR D-TYPE TRACK TEST ● BUCCIALI ● BRISTOL V8 PROFILE

TRADITIONAL TRs

CLASSIC CHOICE

If you've enjoyed reading this book, then you're going to love CLASSIC AND SPORTSCAR magazine. Firmly established as the best classic car magazine, both in Britain and overseas, CLASSIC AND SPORTSCAR covers the cars you know and love, the cars you've always dreamed about … and some you've never even heard of!

Each issue contains:
● A *Profile* of a popular classic giving buying, restoration and prices information.
● A *Track Test* by famous historic racer Willie Green.
● A *Back to Back* group test comparison between classics which were rivals in their day.
● Round-up of club activities in *Club Focus*.
● All the exciting old car discoveries in *Worthy*.
● Lovingly photographed features about the world's most exotic cars.

CLASSIC AND SPORTSCAR is published monthly – don't miss it!

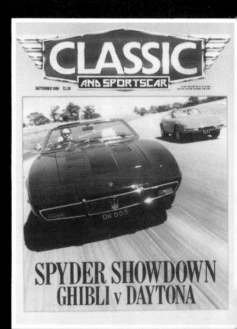

**SPYDER SHOWDOWN
GHIBLI v DAYTONA**

FAB FOUR
ISO v FERRARI v MASERATI v LAMBORGHINI

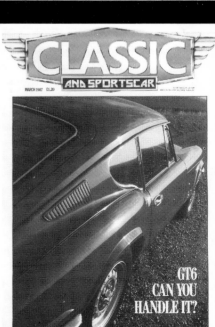

GT6 CAN YOU HANDLE IT?